PEOPLE'S   NICARAGUA

One of several posters explaining the link between education and liberation.

Poster on a wall at the University of Central America, commemorating a former student, martyr of the revolution.

P E O P L E ' S
NICARAGUA

Harry R. Targ

International Publishers, New York

Photographs by Rocio Martinez
Jan Beckstrand
Bob Teclaw
Harry Targ

Front cover, top: Mother with children at the clinic
in San Rafael del Sur
2nd: Javier, former commandante from Jinotega, with
his daughter and another child
Back cover: A session of the women's conference in Jinotega

Library of Congress Cataloging-in-Publication Data

Targ, Harry R.
    People's Nicaragua / Harry R. Targ.
        p.   cm.
    ISBN 0-7178-0675-8 : $5.95
    1. Nicaragua—Politics and government—1979- 2. Nicaragua-
-Description and travel—1987- 3. Targ. Harry R.—Journeys-
-Nicaragua. I. Title.
F1528.T37   1989
972.8505'3—dc20   89-36685
                                                                        CIP

CONTENTS

ACKNOWLEDGEMENTS

Any written work is the summation of a myriad of experiences, inspirations, and supports in an author's life – some very personal, others more broadly historical.

I owe a great debt to those in my personal life who have provided me with love and encouragement: my wife Dena B. Targ and my parents Genevieve and Irving Targ. While she arrived later, my daughter Rebecca has added to that love and renewed my optimism about youthful commitments to social change.

I must make particular note of the important role played by Willie Ney in providing me with one of my greatest life experiences, the trip to Nicaragua. Willie is another young person who gives one hope about the future. His total commitment to the Nicaraguan people in their struggle is a model for others to emulate. Without him, Indiana citizens would be far less informed about, or active in supporting, the struggles of the Nicaraguan people over the last five years.

I wish to note the warm supportive relationship that I have shared with my dear friends Bob Teclaw and Jan Beckstrand during the trip and since. I have also become more acquainted with Rocio Martinez and have been inspired by her commitment of solidarity to Latin American peoples.

Finally, I must record my admiration for the people of Nicaragua, who in all their adversity remain committed to progressive social change, and despite the murderous policies of the United States government remain warm and compassionate toward its citizens. I hope that in some small way the portrait of their struggles, their hopes, their visions, presented in this book will contribute to greater public opposition here to our government's blockade, and its military and political sabotage of the government of the People's Nicaragua.

Harry R. Targ

The countryside viewed from a hill in La Esperanza. Note the dugout in foreground, where guards can hide protected and watch for contra raiders.

Jan, at left, with patients and staff; health post at Los Chiles

Plaza of the Revolution, facing the National Parliament. In the foreground, the eternal flame in memory of Carlos Fonseca, Sandinista founder.

CHAPTER ONE

Nicaragua and U.S. Imperialism

Few people travel to another land without some sense of what they will see, some idea about the country's place in the broader historical, political and economic system in which it exists. This is especially so for people who visit a land like Nicaragua not only to learn but to gain experience for political purposes back home. And all this applied to the visit I made to Nicaragua with two close friends in June 1987. We toured up and down the west coast of the country and spent time along the Rio San Juan on the Costa Rican border.

Let me first place the trip in the broad political and economic context of the epoch in which we live, and give you some notion of our political predispositions as we embarked on our tour. In most cases, we found confirmation of our historical and political perspectives, but the tour also provided opportunities to find evidence to challenge the predispositions, if such evidence existed.

The United States in Nicaragua

U.S. involvement in Nicaragua began as early as the 1840s, when the Vanderbilts and other entrepreneurs began to use the Central American isthmus in expediting transportation between the east and west coasts of the United States. California gold provided the impetus for this growing interest in a transcontinental route, and the United States began plans to construct a canal that would link the Caribbean with the Pacific Ocean via the Rio San Juan, which flows most of the way across Nicaragua and connects with Lake Nicaragua.

North American control was extended when an American adventurer, William Walker, organized an army to invade and conquer Nicaragua. Walker was successful for a time (1855-57), until a Central American army, outraged by the effrontery of North American occupation of a neighboring country, ousted him before he was able to complete the creation of a new empire in the region.

1

Though it ended in ignominious defeat, the Walker episode was a prelude to much more extensive interventionism. Jose Santos Zelaya, president from 1893 to 1909, sought to construct an autonomous capitalist system in Nicaragua, a project that conflicted with the U.S. need to maintain all of Central America in economic dependency. Consequently, U.S. marines were sent to Nicaragua in 1909 to help opponents of Zelaya expel him from office. In 1912, with U.S. interests still being challenged, the marines returned to establish stability in the country. This time they stayed for much of the following twenty years.

In 1927, General Augusto Cesar Sandino organized a guerrilla army to eject the U.S. marines from his country. Thus began a six-year war that culminated in the victory of Sandino's forces. Facing this nationalist army on the ground in Nicaragua and the growing opposition to U.S. interventionism at home, the colossus of the north pulled its forces out in 1933. Before the U.S. marines left, however, they installed Anastasio Somoza Garcia as head of the new Nicaraguan National Guard. From this position, the U.S.-sponsored Somoza was able to consolidate his power, first having Sandino assassinated. By 1936, Somoza was Nicaragua's president.

From 1936 until 1979, Somoza and his two sons ruled with an iron hand and assumed dominance of the country's economy. The Somoza family dynasty became one of the most brutal dictatorships in Latin America. The U.S. government gave full support to the Somoza regime because of its services to U.S. capitalism in the region, its virulent anti-communism and its military cooperation with U.S. covert operations against progressive states in Central America, including Guatemala in the 1950s and Cuba in the early 1960s. President Franklin Roosevelt is reputed to have said about the senior Somoza, "He is a son-of-a-bitch, but at least he is our son-of-a-bitch."

The Somoza Period

Anastasio Somoza Garcia, founder of the dynasty, held power until assassinated by poet Rigoberto Lopez in 1956. Then Luis Somoza assumed the presidency of the country, and at his death in 1967 the last Somoza, Anastasio Somoza Debayle, assumed full power. Over the course of 43 years, the Somozas accumulated enormous wealth as well as power. By the 1970s they owned 20 percent of all cultivable land, a large number of the commercial businesses and most factories in the country, but in the late 1970s, some members of the country's old economic ruling class and some newer capitalists joined the growing mass movement to oust the last Somoza.

The wealth amassed by the Somoza dynasty, of course, had been taken from the lives of the Nicaraguan masses. Life expectancy for the people was 53 years; 57 percent of the population was illiterate and 22 percent of the people were unemployed. The bottom 50 percent of the population shared 15 percent of the nation's gross domestic product, while the top 5 percent had 30 percent of it. Central to the experience of the Nicaraguan people were enormous poverty, great inequalities in income and wealth, and political powerlessness.

The 1972 earthquake in Nicaragua epitomized the relationship of the Somoza regime to the population at large. The earthquake destroyed 80 percent of Managua, the capital city. Responding to the destruction and human tragedy, agencies and people around the world sent relief funds and supplies. Somoza expropriated the relief funds, even sold blood, and never repaired the battered capital city. This outraged the Nicaraguan people even more than the ongoing conditions and led to the escalation of the guerrilla movement to oust Somoza.

The Revolutionary Struggle

The Sandinista National Liberation Front (FSLN) had been formed in 1961 by progressive Nicaraguans who sought to organize a mass movement to force the Somoza dynasty from power. Over the course of a decade the movement experienced. some gains, but also suffered many defeats as it sought by all sorts of means, including organized guerrilla war, to oust the regime.

By the 1970s, the years of struggle, sacrifice and death began to pay off. Thousands of Nicaraguans joined the struggle. Included were Christian activists imbued with the spirit of liberation theology, university students, peasants, workers and – as the decade advanced – members of the bourgeoisie.

Between 1977 and 1979, the mass movement was forced to engage in armed struggle and the nation was engulfed in a bloody civil war. Somoza unleashed his National Guard on urban and rural populations, increasingly used torture and even bombed large concentrations of people. Of a population of 2.5 million, 40,000 were killed in the struggle and 100,000 wounded. U.S. citizens became aware of the war in 1979 when an American television reporter was killed by a National Guardsman.

Somoza was forced to flee in July 1979, and on July 19 the FSLN armies marched triumphantly into Managua, proclaiming a new era for the people. But the country was physically devastated and financially bankrupt. Only two months earlier, Nicaragua had received a $1.6 million loan from the International Monetary Fund (IMF), endorsed by the United States. Along with his family riches, Somoza took much of this money with him when he left the country.

The first five years of the revolution, from July 1979 to 1983, brought much constructive change in the lives of the Nicaraguan people. It was a period of revolutionary enthusiasm as the government experimented with new educational, medical and agricultural policies. Within two years, 40,000 landless peasant families received land. (Now, 60 percent of all peasant families have land.) During the first five years, corn production increased by 10 percent and bean production by 45 percent; rice production doubled. Food consumption of these items increased by between 30 and 40 percent.

The infant mortality rate was cut by one-third and the incidence of malaria declined by 50 percent as a result of the bold, effective, new health campaigns. Also, one million Nicaraguans were inoculated against polio, measles and tetanus. The World Health Organization and UNICEF gave Nicaragua awards for best health achievements in the Third World.

The new government engaged in a large-scale educational program involving virtually the entire country. The first priority was a literacy campaign in which thousands of young people moved to the countryside to teach peasants how to read and write. In the course of one year, illiteracy dropped from 50 percent to 14 percent. The government has continued to provide education, including adult education, throughout the country and received an award from UNESCO for the 1980 literacy campaign.

Enormous problems faced the new government. They were the result of the historic economic dependency of the Nicaraguan economy on international capitalism and the plundering of the economy by the Somoza family. To this underdevelopment was added the devastation of the civil war. Consequently, the needs of the people for basic foodstuffs, health and education were monumental. The Sandinista-led government acted on those needs and was experiencing some level of success in meeting them when the U.S.-sponsored war against the Nicaraguan people escalated.

U.S. Foreign Policy Toward Nicaragua in the 1980s

After World War II, American capitalism seized the opportunity to establish its powerful presence around the globe. U.S. trade, foreign investment, control over valuable resources and access to cheap labor reinforced U.S. economic might, at the expense of much of the world.

However, by the 1960s, the distribution of power and wealth in the global political economy had begun to change. A Socialist bloc had established its permanence, and many regimes outside this bloc had come to power calling themselves Socialist. The Third World rapidly decolonized; new regimes demanded changes in the way the capitalist-controlled world economy operated. Further, European and Japanese capital had been revitalized and were able to challenge the U.S. position in the global economy. Finally, liberation movements were growing all around the periphery of the capitalist world economy.

The combined weight of these challenges meant the declining relative power of the United States – economically, politically and militarily. The United States could not impose its political will on other countries as it had during the height of its hegemony, when it success-fully crushed regimes in Iran and Guatemala in the 1950s, and invaded the Dominican Republic in the 1960s to forestall a nationalist from coming to power.

The challenges to the U.S. position in the world became acute by the 1970s, and despite U.S. success in ousting from Chile the govern-ment of Salvador Allende, the most significant foreign policy issue of the decade was the U.S. loss of the war in Vietnam. Both the Carter and the Reagan-Bush administrations set out to overcome the loss of U.S. power, prestige and economic presence in the world.

This background on U.S. foreign policy is important to help understand our policy toward Nicaragua in the 1970s and 1980s. As the civil war there was escalating in 1978, the Carter administration was faced with the dilemma of deciding how to respond to the possible loss of one of the closest friends of the United States in the Western Hemisphere.

Carter attempted to convince Somoza to leave office and appoint a replacement as chief of state, to defuse the crisis before the revolu-tionaries could come to power. Somoza refused to resign, and Carter continued to support his regime, even authorizing the IMF loan to the Nicaraguan government shortly before the end of Somoza's "reign."

In June 1979, Carter made a last minute attempt to forestall the coming to power of the FSLN-led movement by proposing an organiza-tion of American States peacekeeping force. Latin American nations refused to endorse the plan because they saw it as an attempt to keep the revolution from succeeding. With this OAS rejection, the Carter administration could only wait and see what would result after Somoza was defeated.

After July 19, 1979, the Carter administration recommended to Congress a $75 million aid package to Nicaragua. It was hoped that by continuing to give some support to the new government, the more conservative and business forces would retain their influence. At the same time, Carter authorized $1 million to help train and support a small force of former Somoza National Guardsmen who were beginning to assemble throughout Central America to fight against the new government. The bulk of the training and support for this new counter-revolutionary army came from the military government of Argentina.

The Reagan-Bush Administration came into office with the goal of overthrowing the new government, as expressed in the Republican party's platform in 1980. One of President Reagan's first diplomatic acts was to cancel the last installment of the $75 million aid commitment.

Reagan then instituted a policy of opposing loans to Nicaragua from international agencies such as the IMF, the International Bank for Reconstruction and Development (World Bank) and the Inter-American Development Bank. The object was to close off all such sources of funding to the new regime.

Those European and Latin American governments that had begun to provide substantial assistance to Nicaragua were pressured by Reagan to end their support for the new regime. During the first five years of the revolution, about 75 percent of Nicaragua's assistance came from these allies of the United States, but after 1983, the pressure on the allied governments bore fruit and assistance to Nicaragua dwindled.

President Reagan also authorized a dramatic increase in support for the then small counterrevolutionary army. He made it clear that the United States would train and finance the contras, most of them former National Guardsmen in the Somoza regime. Later, the contra leadership would continue to be former Somozistas, from either the National Guard or the wealthy class of Nicaragua.

The Reagan-Bush administration authorized Central Intelligence Agency (CIA) covert operations in support of the contras, such as mining Nicaragua's harbors, blowing up bridges, funneling arms to the contras and training them to engage in terror campaigns against the country's rural population. Reagan dramatically escalated the U.S. military occupation of Central America, thoroughly militarizing Honduras; arming, training and fighting along with the military forces of El Salvador; and pressuring Costa Rica to increase its police and internal defense forces.

On the diplomatic front, the Reagan-Bush administration continued to pressure Latin and European nations to withdraw their support from Nicaragua; Western aid and support were reduced. Since military and economic aid were necessary for survival, Nicaragua sought more help from Socialist countries. Then the Reagan-Bush administration raised the specter of the "Soviet threat" in Central America to rationalize the military and economic policy that had created the above chain of events.

Latin American nations, from 1982 on, sought to negotiate a solution of the crises in Central America. The Contadora countries

(Mexico, Venezuela, Panama and Colombia) were able to develop a peace treaty involving the five Central American countries (El Salvador, Honduras, Nicaragua, Guatemala and Costa Rica) but the United States refused to agree to its central provisions that called for the withdrawal of all external military forces from Central America.

When the Nicaraguan government held elections in 1984, in which seven parties participated, the U.S. administration, rather than encouraging the move to electoral democracy, damned the elections as fraudulent. Outside observers claimed that the election was reasonably fair and open and was considerably more democratic in its procedure than the two recent elections in El Salvador, where violence precluded the participation of the broad opposition movement.

Finally, what hurt almost as much as the war was the Reagan decision in 1985 to institute a full embargo against the Nicaraguan government, in violation of international law and broadly accepted trade agreements. Nicaraguan goods could no longer be sold in the United States, and the Nicaraguans could no longer buy the spare parts that were so important to the entire industrial and transportation infrastructure because of the country's historical dependency on the United States.

This policy toward Nicaragua was very similar to U.S. policies in the past toward Iran, Guatemala, the Dominican Republic, Chile, Cuba, Jamaica, Indonesia, Angola, Mozambique, 'Ghana, Algeria and other countries that had asserted their right to national self-determination. Many Latin Americans see the Nicaraguan revolution as a mass-based movement that overthrew a ruthless dictator closely allied to the United States.

For most Nicaraguans, the Somoza dynasty was inextricably tied to the capitalist political economy, and their country's underdevelopment was a by-product of this relationship. By ousting Somoza, they were also taking a stand against U.S. economic, political and military domination. This the Carter and Reagan-Bush administrations felt the need to oppose. If others in the region saw success in Nicaragua, they too would seek their own liberation.

The Contras

Many members of the Somoza National Guard fled Nicaragua as the Sandinista-led movement assumed power in July 1979. Hundreds, if not thousands, traveled to Guatemala, Honduras or the United States. Some became robbers and terrorists in neighboring countries. Military personnel from Argentina began to train exiled guardsmen, hoping to form a counterrevolutionary army to retake Nicaragua. The Carter administration provided about one million dollars to support this effort.

When President Reagan came into office, he committed the U.S. government to the construction of a contra army to harass – if not destroy – the revolution; the first large allocation of funds was $19 million. Leading this new army were almost entirely former Somozistas. A 1985 Congressional report found that 46 of the top 48 contra leaders were former members of the Somoza National Guard.

After 1982, the contra war escalated. Stationed to the north of Nicaragua in Honduras and to the south in Costa Rica, bands of contras carried out terrorist raids against Nicaraguan rural settlements. At first the Reagan-Bush administration said it was supporting the contras to interdict the flow of arms from Nicaragua to the rebels in El Salvador. However, the administration was never able to document any such flow of arms, and as the war escalated, that rationale was heard less and less. It became clear to U.S. citizens and foreigners alike that the intent was to bleed the Nicaraguan economy and society.

Given the continuing opposition of the American people to that policy, the U.S. Congress introduced prohibitions against using U.S. funds to overthrow the Nicaraguan government. Even though it was exceedingly unlikely that the contras could ever achieve victory in Nicaragua, the Reagan-Bush administration tried to get funds, even private funds from virulent anti-communist fringe groups, to keep the contras operating and make the Nicaraguan people suffer. Over time, it was felt, the suffering would cause the Nicaraguan government to lose its base of support.

Consequently, a small and ineffective fighting force of some 8,000 to 10,000 contras was kept alive, mostly along the Honduran border. Their primary military activity involved terrorist attacks against isolated rural settlements. They targeted health clinics, schools and rural agricultural cooperatives for destruction, and killed thousands of teachers, medical personnel and agricultural and engineering specialists working in the countryside. The contras have been accused by virtually every human rights group of engaging in terror, violence and economic sabotage.

In 1986, the U.S. Congress authorized $100 million for the contras, the largest single congressional authorization of support since 1980. With this major funding, there was pressure on the contras to show some success to justify continued support, and in 1986 and 1987 a large percentage of them began to infiltrate into Nicaragua. With their increased presence inside the country, and the establishment of CIA supply drops to them, the war escalated dramatically. There were contra raids in large areas of northern Nicaragua, and some in the central part of the country. As 1987 proceeded, some military activity resumed along the Costa Rican border, where it had almost completely stopped in 1985.

The escalated contra attacks in 1987 required massive allocations of resources to fight them and by that summer, 55 percent of Nicaragua's budget was being allocated for the war. The U.S. media heralded the new contra military activity and happily portrayed the increasing problems for the government, but in no case were there any military or political actions that showed contra success. They could not establish any permanent presence or win support among the people in any populated area of the country. They could only destroy and kill.

In August 1987, the presidents of the five Central American countries signed a peace treaty at Esquipulas in Guatemala. Among its provisions, the treaty called for an end to outside intervention in support of insurgent forces in the region, government dialogue with internal opposition forces in each country, democratization, and a general movement toward the end of armed conflict.

Despite the peace treaty, violence continued against the people of Nicaragua. In the spring of 1988, as a result of declining Congressional support for the contras and a series of military defeats, some contra leaders signed a peace pact with the Nicaraguan government at Sapoá in southern Nicaragua. Unfortunately, by June 1988, the Reagan-Bush administration had pressured the contras to support the most hardline faction in the conflict-ridden leadership and reneged on prior agreements. As of September 1988, a tenuous military truce was in effect in Nicaragua but was repeatedly being violated by the contras, who had again begun to engage in terror against the people. But about 90 percent of the contra forces, lacking U.S. financial support and suffering military defeats, were back in Honduras.

Economic Decline in Nicaragua Since 1983

The Reagan and Bush administrations have orchestrated an aggressive economic, military and diplomatic offensive against Nicaragua. The economic boycott ended the historical trade, aid and investment relationship between the two countries and made it all but impossible to get spare parts and to sell sugar and coffee to the United States. The war not only required a commitment of more than half the country's budget for defense but almost totally disrupted coffee growing, the major generator of foreign exchange.

The Nicaraguan government had to institute a draft and policy of reserve duty to defend the country. As a result, labor resources became scarce. In addition, in rural cooperatives, agricultural workers had to spend hours on guard duty because the contra's terrorist attacks were destroying the valuable gains made in health, education and agricultural production. And, most critical, the war was killing thousands of Nicaraguan men, women and children.

On the diplomatic front, the Reagan-Bush administration was partially successful in pressuring European and Latin American countries to withdraw economic support for the Nicaraguan government. Also, until the Esquipulas Treaty of August 1987, Reagan was able to blackmail the governments of El Salvador, Honduras and Costa Rica to cooperate in opposing the Nicaraguan government and refusing to work towards a peace settlement. As Nicaragua was forced to seek more support from Socialist countries, the U.S. propaganda mill proclaimed that events in Nicaragua were increasingly a threat to U.S. national interests because of Soviet proximity in the region.

The central point is that the contra war, the economic boycott and the diplomatic attack have severely damaged the economic and political infrastructure of Nicaragua. There are those who argue that Nicaragua's economic problems result from governmental bungling, ideological rigidities and bureaucracy, and that the war and economic blockade are merely excuses. But from 1979 to 1983 there were some substantial successes in economic development and social policy, and it was only after the war escalated that the economic trends worsened.

By 1987, the policy of the Nicaraguan government was to maintain a "war economy," concentrating resources on fighting the contras and maintaining the gains in social and economic change achieved since 1979. Plans for economic development, expanded programs in health and education, and a broadened cultural life would have to await the war's end. On the diplomatic front, every effort was being made to pursue the peace process, to get international pressure on the United States to end its vicious war against the Nicaraguan people.

The Low Intensity Conflict

Central to U.S. foreign policy in the 1980s are the Reagan-Bush Doctrine and its operational arm, "low intensity conflict." The Reagan Doctrine is the administration's stated goal of working toward the overthrow or internal destruction of political regimes around the world that are seen as contrary to U.S. interests and ideology. Since these regimes were generally labeled communist, the central point of the doctrine is to overthrow communist governments that have achieved power.

Many people believe that in the long run, nationalist and socialist movements will achieve power in the Third World, breaking out of the level of impoverishment and powerlessness brought on by their incorporation into the international capitalist system, but for President Reagan the historical agenda included a Third World return to "free" countries, with market economies linked to the United States.

Thus the Reagan Doctrine, now carried forward by the Bush administration, asserts that history is moving in the direction of anti-communism, anti-nationalism and anti-socialism. U.S. policies have been designed to achieve this historic reversal, providing military support for counterrevolutionary forces, such as the contras, who are willing to fight for a return to the old ways of life in their countries.

This policy is referred to as "low intensity" because the administration prefers to support the contras covertly so that the American public only dimly understands what its government is doing. This masking of U.S. policy was required because the American people were said to be suffering from the "Vietnam Syndrome"; that is, they opposed U.S. interventionism. Therefore, to achieve the goals of the Reagan Doctrine despite public opinion, it would be necessary to hire, train, supply, finance and bribe a mercenary army.

If the mercenaries did not succeed in ousting the repugnant regime by military force, pursuing the policy of low intensity conflict would drain the economy and government of the targeted country so that some time in the future the regime might fall for lack of economic or political support.

An additional "positive" outcome, from the standpoint of the administration planners, would be the message that these conflicts send to masses of people in the Third World: If they seek their own liberation they will pay a very heavy price, for the United States will resist with all its massive resources any attempt of a people to secure its own self-determination.

The Nicaraguan people have struggled for political and economic autonomy, and have been made to suffer for their vision as the United States government tries to destroy one of the most exciting experiments in progressive social and economic change in the Third World.

A view of Los Chiles

Shanty construction on vacant land in Managua

CHAPTER TWO

Who Made the Trip and Why

I traveled to Nicaragua with two friends, Bob Teclaw and Jan Beckstrand, and we began our two-week tour under the guidance of Willie Ney, a young man who was active in the movement to bring material aid – funds, clothing, medicines, tools and other needed goods – to the Rio San Juan region. Willie was the facilitator of a fundraising effort by Fort Wayne, Indiana activists to fund and construct an addition to a health clinic in a city known as San Rafael del Sur. The Fort Wayne community raised $32,000, some of which we brought with us to present to administrators of the clinic. Willie had been living in Nicaragua for nine months and had been there off and on for several years. Visiting him was a woman friend from our university, Rocio Martinez. (Later, she would become Willie's wife.)

Bob, Jan and I had met a year earlier at a dinner sponsored by the local Central American solidarity group, the Committee in Solidarity With the People of El Salvador (CISPES). Bob and Jan had just moved to Lafayette, Indiana, he as an assistant professor of veterinary medicine and she as an associate professor of nursing at a university some sixty miles away. They had learned their politics and derived their values from the 1960s, and had spent a year in rural Mexico, where Bob did research for his doctoral dissertation.

After our first meeting, my wife, Dena, encouraged them to participate in CISPES and got Bob to join the local American Federation of Teachers (AFT). Interested in meeting new people and continuing their long-term commitment to social change, they became local activists; Bob particularly so, because he was employed on the Lafayette campus of Purdue University. He began to work with local Central American activists to bring speakers to the community, to raise money for material aid for El Salvador and Nicaragua, and to generate public opposition to the policies of the Reagan-Bush administration toward Central America. When Bob said that he and Jan were seriously planning to go to Nicaragua, we began to explore the idea of going together.

13

This was not the first time I had thought about visiting Nicaragua, but my expressions of interest had never led me to commit myself seriously. Willie, talking with us after a visit to Lafayette, said we should come as his guests; he would guide us through Nicaragua. The Nicaraguan government representative who was touring with Willie also encouraged us to visit her country.

Bob spoke fluent Spanish, and we could have a tour guided by a young, articulate, committed and informed activist, so I thought it was an ideal opportunity and I must take advantage of it, despite mixed feelings.

By April 1987, Bob, Jan and I had made the commitment to go to Nicaragua in May or June of that year and we began the planning: where to purchase airline tickets; what medicines and inoculations to get; what kind of luggage to take, what clothing to bring; what items to bring for people we would meet in the country.

Awaiting the trip, I was driven sometimes by romantic feelings of solidarity with the revolutionary process and the Nicaraguan people, of being part of the world-historic process of change. Other times I was gripped by fears of impending confrontations with contras as we traveled, or of being bitten by snakes, or contracting malaria or – a standard fear whenever I travel – that the plane would crash on the way.

As the time to leave approached, my fears increased so that periodically I would ask myself why I was going at all. Then would come feelings of guilt, feelings that would recur several times in Nicaragua, that I thought more about my own creature comforts and personal safety than about the Nicaraguan people, whose physical and psychological security were being destroyed by U.S. support of the contra war. During calmer moments, before leaving and during the trip, I would remind myself that one's feelings bear less on the real world than one's actions, and it is the latter that can and do affect people for better or worse. I also came to understand how one's class affects one's consciousness. Despite my radical beliefs, I realized that I remained a product of that bourgeois class I so criticized in my political work.

The Trip Begins

We left Lafayette on the evening of Thursday, June 4, and drove to Chicago. Friday morning, we flew to Mexico City. Saturday afternoon we flew from Mexico City to Managua, Nicaragua.

Much to our chagrin, we landed in San Salvador for a short stopover on our way to Managua. I had been lecturing in classes and speaking at political meetings for years about Salvadoran death squads, and there we were, sitting in a Nicaraguan AeroNica plane at the airport in San Salvador. I had fantasies about my importance to revolutionary change in Central America, and hence the danger I faced in that airport, but fortunately, nothing of note occurred there. Bob and I manifested our fears in frivolous laughter and all-too-loud comments about where we were; Jan was angry with us, justly so, for making public asses of ourselves.

Roughly an hour after takeoff from the airport at San Salvador, we landed in Managua in a rainstorm. As we circled the airport we heard a loud banging noise. I assumed lightning had struck on or near the plane; in the general commotion of our impending landing in revolutionary Nicaragua, the full fearful impact of the noise did not register.

We walked to the terminal to begin the process of entering the country. The first stop was at a window where dollars were changed into cordobas. We were required to buy $60 worth of Nicaraguan currency; in the generally skyrocketing inflation, the exchange rate was then 4,000 cordobas per dollar. We received three big bundles of small currency bills, which it was difficult to find a place for. The money would not fit into pockets, billfolds or purses but had to be stuffed into our carry-on luggage. We then proceeded to show our passports to an inspector seated in a glass-enclosed room, and then filed past him to get our luggage and take it to the customs line.

The baggage/customs area was a big hot room filled with the 75 or so travelers who had just arrived and a small staff of examiners. Just in front of me in line were two Nicaraguans returning with many purchases. The couple, clearly wealthy, had four pieces of luggage and several boxes. The young woman customs agent, perhaps 20 years old at most, opened and examined everything – picking and pulling, messing clothes, books, toys and other commodities. I noted with distaste two warfare board games and wondered if they were for children of contra supporters.

The wealthy Nicaraguan man became increasingly angry, while his wife sought to be cheerful and smooth over the growing hostility between him and the customs agent. He urged the agent not to open two boxes, which he said contained computer disks. He appealed to the agent's supervisor, but to no avail. With some pleasure, she broke open the two boxes and roughly rummaged through the enclosed materials. This confrontation was clearly a manifestation of class hatred. conscious of my own class background and my citizenship of Yankee imperialism, I expected my luggage to be wn apart, undershorts thrown across the counter, antacid array next to unpacked T-shirts and toilet paper. But when two pieces of luggage and my backpack on the counter, the ped one piece then placed her hand in it, smiled for the first

CAM

time, and then signaled that I was cleared. This provided me with my first sense of the openness and generosity with which Nicaraguans distinguished between their own wealthy class, murderous contra-supporting gringos, and U.S. citizens who were in solidarity with the Nicaraguan people.

Our guide and friend met us outside the customs room and introduced us to a young Nicaraguan woman who worked in the office of the Managua region. Willie introduced her as an assistant to Daniel Ortega, and she welcomed us officially, which temporarily made us feel important. With her aide, she drove us to the neighborhood of relatively comfortable houses, by Managuan standards, where we were to stay. Bob, Jan and I were to have two rooms in a house owned by an elderly Nicaraguan woman, one she shared with an eight-year-old girl, perhaps a granddaughter. Willie and other solidarity workers lived nearby.

After dropping off our luggage, we went down the street to Willie's house to discuss our two-week schedule. We drank some cola, an increasingly precious commodity, and learned what we would be doing in the exciting days to come. The next day, Sunday, the Nicaraguan woman we had met in Lafayette was giving a party in our honor on an island in Lake Nicaragua near Granada. She was from a wealthy family, and among the guests would be some of her rich friends who were hostile to the Sandinista government. We would meet with governmental officials on Monday, including the woman who welcomed us on our arrival and the Vice Rector of the University of Central America. Tuesday's schedule included meeting a Honduran refugee and visiting a public beachside resort.

On Wednesday we would drive to San Rafael del Sur, 50 kilometers southwest of Managua, to tour a health clinic and other facilities in a town receiving material aid from Indiana communities. Thursday we would tour Salvadoran refugee cooperatives in and around Managua. Friday, Saturday and Sunday we would be traveling north to a city called Jinotega, in the province of the same name, just miles from the contra war. The following Monday, Willie and I had plans to return to San Rafael del Sur to visit a sugar refinery and meet with leaders of the union locals there. From Tuesday to Friday of that week we would go to the Rio San Juan along the Costa Rican border, to visit rural cooperatives as well as receive information about economic development in the entire region. Friday would be spent visiting with an advisor to Daniel Ortega and in preparation for our return to Mexico City and the United States. So, with a multitude of fears and questions, we retired for the night. It seemed incredible that I was actually in revolutionary Nicaragua, ready to embark on the most powerful political experience of my life.

I had come a long way from my emerging state of political consciousness in the late 1950s, that culturally homogenized and politically repressed decade. As a journalism and political science student in 1959 and 1960, I had begun to look with favor upon Adlai Stevenson's third attempted presidential candidacy. When that failed, I gradually developed enthusiasm for the Kennedy candidacy, somewhat moved by his calls for a spirit of sacrifice and commitment to social change. These inklings of an emerging political consciousness were very much affected by the liberal and humane values communicated by my parents and their general orientation toward candidates of the Democratic Party, though they themselves were not politically active.

Until about 1967 I remained a liberal politically, but Dena, a college activist at Roosevelt University, inspired in me a much greater sympathy for the tactics as well as the goals of the civil rights movement, and by the late 1960s we had moved to the left.

A profound, consciousness-shaping experience was the Vietnam War; particularly so in my case because I was in the National Guard reserves, where the threat of activation to full-time military duty increased as the war escalated. As a graduate student in political science and a prospective foot soldier, my interest in, concern about and opposition to that war escalated markedly; by the time I came to my academic position at Purdue University in 1967, I vowed to work against the war as best I could. Such were the beginnings of my political work, to continue off and on ever since.

One of my teaching tasks – I teach international relations, U.S. foreign policy and U.S. political economy primarily – was to make sense of the Vietnam War. As did many analysts, I began with the liberal critic's wisdom that U.S. policy was mistakenly shaped by a virulent anti-communism; the United States had made "mistakes" in countries like Guatemala and Iran because we saw communism where it did not really exist. U.S. policy was naive, misguided and erroneously conditioned by the irrationalities of American politics, particularly McCarthyism, but wise leadership could change its character. If only we could convince our leaders of the folly of their ways, we liberal critics thought, the United States could become a beacon of hope to the world.

A more sophisticated kind of liberal critique of U.S. foreign policy captured my imagination for a time; it held that the United States should behave like all powerful states, should seek to maximize its power in a world of fear and insecurity. This approach articulated a view that national interest rather than messianic purpose should be the guide to policy. The mistake that was being made by U.S. policymakers, these "realist" writers claimed, was that they acted in the world on the basis of universal principles that other nations might not share; we developed simplistic visions of the world in a struggle between "us" and "them," trying to get the country to act out crusades, making the world safe for democracy or rolling back communism. The project of the foreign policy critic, therefore, was to convince the leaders that a realistic foreign policy based upon national interest, balances of power, spheres of influence and secret diplomacy was more likely to help the country achieve its goals than mountaintop proclamations to masses of followers on how the United States will save the world.

However, as I prepared lectures on international relations and foreign policy, I began to see that the notion that America's statesmen were misguided, befogged with blind anti-communist sentiments, and arrogant in their fundamental "rightness" was too narrow a frame of reference for understanding U.S. foreign policy. Of course, my own teaching and political consciousness were being shaped by the struggles in the streets and on campuses around the nation, along with the particular campus battles in which I had some role.

What seemed clear was that the "mistakes" of Vietnam were similar to the "mistakes" in Greece in the 1940s, when the United States intervened to support a crypto-fascist regime threatened with defeat by a popular movement; or in Korea, where the United States fought a long, bloody war to keep in power a corrupt anti-Communist politician, Syngman Rhee, contrary to the interests of the Korean people whether north or south of the 38th parallel. These "mistakes" had also occurred in Iran and Guatemala, with the United States intervening covertly to overthrow governments deemed to be tilting toward communism. These "mistakes" marred relations with Cuba, as the United States created an armed interventionary force in 1960 to attempt the ouster of Fidel Castro. Similarly, the United States sent 22,000 marines to "protect" American citizens and to "save" the Dominican Republic from communism. The follies of supporting dictatorships in Taiwan, Spain, South Korea, South Africa and Brazil seemed to stem less from misguided policies than from a pattern of supporting the status quo and political repression, mainly to serve U.S. economic interests. U.S. policy, the newer revisionist historians argued, was guided by the needs of capitalism to secure sites for foreign investment, cheap labor, markets and raw materials, and it was those features that these "mistakes" had in common.

My gradual awakening to a new outlook on American political life and foreign policy was also stimulated by a reexamination of the backgrounds and interests of those who make policy. The liberal view held that irrespective of their backgrounds, the most important thing about our political leaders was their misguided fear of a universal communist menace. Their outlooks were flawed, based on the tradition of red-baiting and the xenophobic fear of communism in American life that goes back to a time even before the Bolshevik revolution.

The radical view of the country's foreign policy leadership argues that they are not misguided, or fools, or dupes of popular culture. Virtually every top decisionmaker in the State Department, Defense Department, Central Intelligence Agency, etc., has roots among and ties to those who own or control the means of production, the bankers and corporate executives. Along with them are the Wall Street lawyers, foundation presidents, university administrators and others who by virtue of background, economic interconnections, wealth and power serve the ruling class in America. Of course, at lower levels of the foreign policy bureaucracy are selected businessmen and academics, and some career diplomats like George Kennan.

The character of U.S. foreign policy was being shaped by those who had particular economic interests and who had their specific vision of what the United States and the world ought to be like. Their global vision featured capitalism as the economic system, and saw American capitalism, particularly, as shaping the world. Nations, peoples and movements who disagreed with this world vision would have to be challenged and ultimately eliminated. The U.S. foreign policy establishment felt it was necessary to marshall the nation's resources for a long-term struggle against the enemies of U.S. economic interests.

But most Americans do not share the wealth and power of those dominating the foreign policy process, so they will not give support to a crusade obviously designed to preserve the wealthy. Rather, there ould have to be some appeal to the humane values of the culture, so the struggle was defined as being against international monolithic communism, a communism that would – in the words of the propagandists – end freedom, crush religion and do all sorts of barbaric things (destroy families, take people's children from them, etc.).

The American ruling establishment also needed support from people in other countries, but unfettered capitalism was not seen by large numbers of them as the best way to achieve human dignity and economic well-being. The United States had to identify the supporters of the American way, a minority usually found among the wealthy and powerful, privileged few. Once identified, the foreign policy task was to put them in power and keep them there. In every administration, beginning with the Truman years, U.S. resources were used to oust from power those leaders who did not fully subscribe to the vision of a world of unfettered capitalism, or who, serving a variety of domestic constituencies, would modify the capitalist systems under their control to meet local needs and demands.

Consequently, those like myself who slowly shifted our thinking from the liberal to the radical view began to see the need to act in opposition to the policies of our own government as it punished other peoples, and to work towards transforming our own society rather than merely pressuring our "misguided" leaders along the path of reason. The issue was conflict between classes and interests over the power of the state; not discourse among rational men.

This new perspective, of course, did not mean that rational discourse, research, writing, debating were not relevant. The marshalling of arguments and evidence, and rigorous theory were all the more needed to convince those who had not reflected enough on the causes underlying policy. Public education and rational discourse were also needed, but had to be directed toward the people, the ultimate force for change.

The late 1960s and early 1970s were a time of intellectual and political ferment for many people. I learned from my wife, my friends, several of the student peace activists on campus and from the declarations and actions of the liberation movements around the world.

However, after the great waves of protest against the Vietnam War and the war itself ended, the movement on our campus and around the nation dwindled and so did my political activity. The period from 1974 to 1980 was a time of reflection and study more than action. The campus where I worked was not traditionally an active one and it did not sustain activities in periods of calm, so I had time to begin to read Marx and others from the Marxist tradition. I found compelling the historical analysis and historically contingent character of political action suggested by the Marxian method. I began to work with midwest scholar/activists who organized Marxist Scholars Conferences and the Marxist Educational Press. I also began to develop an interest in U.S. labor history, which led me to a past replete with action, commitment and struggles for social change. In the 1960s, my historical frame of reference usually had not gone beyond the day before yesterday. Learning of one's roots and the continuity of struggles for change is a powerful tool, both as inspiration and as a guide to action. In this regard, Central American peoples have a much better understanding of their histories than progressive North Americans.

While studying Marx and labor history, and reflecting on the need for political change in the United States, I provided written materials and funds for a colleague who was a leader of an opposition socialist party in the Bahamas. Another friend and I constituted ourselves a two-person support committee for the Bahamas, and I made a five-day trip there, meeting with government, church and business leaders and spending most of my time "over the hill" in the Black working-class community. I had the opportunity to speak at the party's headquarters, discussing the nature of the modern global political economy.

The Bahamas visit provided me with my first "Third World" experience. (Later I reflected often on how developed the islands were compared to Nicaragua.) I was particularly inspired by the level of commitment and political knowledge of the working people, their practical experience with the realities of power, struggle and exploitation, and their appreciation of the possibilities for social change – something totally lacking among most academics. I began to research and write about the political economy of imperialism in the Caribbean, with particular attention to the Bahamas and Jamaica.

The Bahamas visit occurred the first week of January, 1981. This was a time when news about El Salvador was just beginning to reach the U.S. press. Four U.S. nuns were raped and murdered in El Salvador by military personnel in December, 1980. In early 1981 two U.S. AFL-CIO representatives who were in El Salvador advising the government on land reform were assassinated in a San Salvador hotel. Hundreds of Salvadoran citizens were being killed each month by rightwing death squads. President Carter had provided military aid to El Salvador; it was suspended after the murder of the nuns, but within a month was resumed to forestall the victory of a guerrilla-led insurrection. I began to look more intently upon what seemed to be an escalating U.S. involvement in El Salvador. Vietnam was in the back of my mind.

A close friend, Bob Perrucci, and I talked off and on about forming a group to articulate opposition to the U.S. role in El Salvador. Together with a woman who had organized a human rights rally for Amnesty International on the anniversary of the assassination of Archbishop Oscar Romero – the Salvadoran leader who had called for an end to U.S. military aid – we called a meeting that some 25 people attended. We soon agreed to a set of principles that emphasized our opposition to U.S. intervention in Central America, and began a campaign of public education that included speakers, literature tables, petitioning and demonstrations.

CISPES

In a progressive bookstore in Chicago, I met the midwest representative of CISPES, and I brought information about the organization back to Lafayette. After some discussion, our group agreed to sponsor a slide show on the history of El Salvador and the struggle then raging. Some time later the Lafayette group agreed to affiliate with the national organization.

The Lafayette CISPES then began a campaign of public education about the nature of U.S. support for repressive regimes in El Salvador and sponsored some events concerning Nicaragua, Guatemala and Honduras. During our first year, we distributed literature about El Salvador, sponsored a Salvadoran speaker representing the Democratic Revolutionary Front (FDR) and the Farabundo Marti Liberation Movement (FMLN), showed documentary films on the struggle and participated in a protest march in Chicago in opposition to the growing U.S. involvement in El Salvador.

After a while, attendance at meetings declined and we found that organizing the small meetings was taking our energies away from the primary work of planning and carrying out public events. This was particularly true as several student activists graduated or withdrew from the group. Some initial activists withdrew and built an active Amnesty International chapter, in part motivated by discomfort with our public support for the FMLN/FDR, who by 1982 were engaged in a civil war with the military junta and the then "elected" government in El Salvador. Bob Perrucci and I continued to organize events and raise money for El Salvador each year since 1982, with the help of two or three campus church people and students; events and money raising were usually successful. Our efforts were visible well beyond what could be expected from our numbers.

We worked on and off campus, and twice the local Northwest Central Labor Council (to which I was an AFT delegate) cosponsored events bearing on trade unions in El Salvador. We became part of a communications network with other Central America groups around the state and the Midwest, and also met with representatives of the FDR/FMLN. Our understanding of the political and class forces and the current state of the civil war was heightened by these interactions. We were particularly impressed with the depth of knowledge, analytical skills and commitment of the Salvadorans we met. They made it clear they were engaged in a historic struggle against one hundred years of political repression and economic exploitation.

In 1986, CISPES and Indiana University faculty and students collaborated to bring the Nicaraguan Ambassador, Carlos Tunnerman, to Purdue. About six hundred people came to hear the ambassador talk, and he was well received.

That spring was a time of flowering activism; some twenty persons joined CISPES and worked selflessly to raise money and educate Lafayette and Purdue citizens. CISPES even elected officers, all students, and carried out a telephone campaign to raise funds for medical and agricultural purposes in rural Salvadoran areas. Some $2,400 was raised, the eighth highest amount for any Midwest city or town affiliated with CISPES.

Unfortunately, when the fall of 1987 approached, most of the previous year's activists had left the university. Bob Perrucci and I, founders of the organization, and Bob Teclaw, who had become a critical force in it, were too accustomed to relying on student activism. For the 1987-88 academic year, we had to commit ourselves to a greater role in the organization, working with some five or six activists to organize public educational events and raise modest sums of money in support of humanitarian projects in El Salvador and Nicaragua.

On reflection, it seems that over the past 25 years I have become more and more politicized and radicalized, with a fuller commitment to the labor movement, as evidenced by my work with the Northwest Central Labor Council, particularly editing its newsletter, and my work with friends to study the impacts of plant closings on working people's lives. Now added was a permanent commitment to the Central American solidarity movement. I suspect my development from liberal Democrat to Marxist-oriented radical was similar to that of thousands of people who had experienced the 1960s and been emotionally and intellectually affected by the Vietnam War.

U.S. foreign policy did not revert to benign internationalism after Vietnam; it continued its expansionist course. U.S. policy in Central America had been foreshadowed in Greece, Korea, Iran, Guatemala, the Dominican Republic, Chile and Grenada.

Obviously, a two-week trip to Nicaragua does not make one an expert, but it can enhance a reality only partially understood through books, lectures and visual aids, and can provide an additional emotional and intellectual grasp of the subject. Going there is not better than other ways of understanding the subject but it *is* an additional means. It may not be insignificant that most major decision-makers involved in the U.S. war against Central America, like Colonel Ollie North and Presidents Reagan and Bush, have spent virtually no time in Nicaragua or El Salvador. Those who have been there stayed mostly in the luxury hotels, like many journalists for the major newspapers and radio or television networks. Our travels around Nicaragua gave us insights we could not gain in any other way.

A two-week trip – modest an experience as it is – allows one to come home and publicly discourse on what one saw. Many audiences – before listening to what someone has to say – want to know whether the speaker has been to the country under discussion. In a media-dominated political world, going to Nicaragua makes one "newsworthy." In the eyes of many people, our two weeks there gave us a special kind of authority and increased our right to be heard about the inspirations and disappointments, the joys and tragedies, and the strengths and weaknesses of the Nicaraguan revolution. The pages that follow provide some glimpses of what we saw and how we saw it.

North Americans protest across the street from the U.S. Embassy, Managua.

CHAPTER THREE

Sights and Sounds of Managua

We arrived at the Nicaraguan airport on a Saturday evening after dark. It rained lightly as we were driven to the barrio where we would stay. Because of the moonless sky and lack of street lights, we saw little of the city as we whisked past people waiting for buses and rides. Managua would remain a mystery until the next day.

Unable to sleep past six or seven in the morning, Bob and I dressed upon awakening shortly after sunrise and began a walk through the nearby streets. We were in a tropical country, very different from home. We passed stucco houses that seemed occupied by Nicaraguans of relatively high income. We also passed a large school, and a big, attractive church that was still locked. Grass and weeds grew wild adjacent to the houses; between the rows of houses were large rock-filled areas that seemed unkempt, not at all like the landscapes of suburban tract housing in the United States.

At the entrance to our street was a gravestone commemorating a revolutionary martyr. We would see many signs of physical destruction, such as the empty rock-filled lots, and many memorials to martyrs, since Somoza had engaged in massive bombings and scorched-earth policies.

Even at seven in the morning, the heat was becoming uncomfortable. The heat and humidity in Managua and along the tropical Rio San Juan would become close to unbearable for "gringos" used to a more temperate climate and air conditioning. In the mountains of the North, in Jinotega, it would be refreshingly cool. Did we prefer to be in that war zone, where it was cool, or to be relatively far from the contras – in Managua and on the Costa Rican border – and swelter? A tough choice.

A Day With the Wealthy

Sunday, our first full day in Nicaragua, we would become acquainted with some of the characteristics of the country's wealthy class.

Sonia Garcia worked for the Nicaraguan government, coordinating solidarity relationships between North Americans and Nicaragua. We had met her two months earlier on her U.S. tour organized by our guide, Willie. She had been married to a member of the wealthy Chamorro family, and when she spoke about the Nicaraguan revolution at Purdue University classes and in a public forum, her audiences were impressed because she was clearly a bourgeois supporter of the revolution. Her brother-in-law, Pedro Chamorro, had been editor of *La Prensa,* and had been gunned down by Somoza supporters in 1978. Unlike many of her friends and family, she had committed herself to the revolution – a commitment, she said, that led to her social isolation.

She had organized a party for us on a small island she owned in Lake Nicaragua, where she had a summer house. A stone's throw from her island were others owned by various wealthy families, many of them Chamorros.

We assembled at her Managua house at about eleven a.m., met some of the other guests and, in several cars, began our journey. Access to the island was by small motor boats from the old colonial city, Granada, about forty miles from Managua. Our drive there gave us our first panoramic view of Managua and the Nicaraguan countryside.

In Granada, we had time to walk around the town square and down some city streets, and we visited the elegant old cathedral adjacent to the town park. Most buildings were of white stucco, somewhat faded and dirty, but Granada impressed us as a city of some elegance and charm. It had been partially destroyed by the North American pirate William Walker in the 1850s. Later in the nineteenth century, it had been the center of activities of the old Nicaraguan Conservative Party, which represented the agricultural oligarchs.

Lake Nicaragua is the country's largest lake (allegedly the only body of fresh water to have sharks). We drove through Granada's lake-front park to the docks and boarded a small motorized boat that could accommodate some fifteen people. After a twenty-minute ride, we landed at Sonia's island.

She had invited a puzzling variety of guests, representing some very contradictory political positions. I could converse only in English, so it was later in the evening that I learned from my Spanish-speaking friends just who was for or against whom in the country's politics. Among the guests were two psychologists from Cuba who were in Nicaragua for a few weeks, an actress from Bluefields who was a supporter of the revolution, a U.S. academic philosopher from Indiana University whom I knew, a young man who was a government economist and three of Sonia's friends.

The day was spent eating, talking and singing; given my language deficiencies, I did little of the latter two. One of Sonia's friends sang and played the guitar and Bob approached me about our singing some U.S. labor songs. While we were both reluctant to sing, we thought our participation would be a contribution to this progressive – I thought – folk fest. I had assumed they were all supporters of the revolution, as was Sonia. But when we began to sing "Solidarity Forever," the music stopped and Sonia's guests began talking with each other, ignoring us. I had the sense that they had no interest in singing progressive songs.

Later, while we were driving home with Willie, I got into a heated discussion about the utility of members of the bourgeoisie serving the revolution. I argued then and still believe that wealthy and middle-class supporters of the revolution should not be ostracized if they contribute their time, energies and resources to bringing about social change for the vast majority of the population. It is not only workers and peasants who have the capacity to be revolutionaries; anyone, whatever his or her class background, can be valuable to society if he/she so chooses.

My compatriots argued that Sonia's friends were damning the revolution during the course of the afternoon discussion (and perhaps the singing as well). Apparently I had misread my small conversations with some of the women in English, and had not sensed the intensity of their negative feelings about the 1979 revolution.

We wondered why the unusual mix of persons had been invited: Cubans, solidarity workers from the United States, government officials, and persons opposed to the Sandinista-led government. Was Sonia interested in exposing us to a variety of class and political perspectives or – given her own class background – were her own associations of this contradictory sort?

On this, our first full day in Nicaragua, we had seen complete freedom of political discourse at the party. The vigorous opposition to the government displayed by some, in front of others just as vigorous in supporting it, put the lie to the Reagan-Bush image of Nicaragua as a totalitarian country. This party was just one of countless indicators, wherever we visited, that there were no constraints on political dialogue. In fact, we had already noted the variety of political and religious graffiti on walls along the main streets in the downtown area of Granada. Nicaragua is a country of contrasts in class, wealth and opinion.

Back to Managua

We spent our second day meeting with university and government officials in Managua and seeing some significant symbols of the 1979 revolution. The first stop was at the University of Central America. We visited Father Arguello, the vice rector of UCA, who was gathering materials to construct a graduate program in international studies. I brought him some materials on the study of international relations and some sample college catalogues describing programs at U.S. universities.

The University of Central America is an attractive but resource-poor urban Jesuit university serving some 2,000 students. As in many Third World nations experiencing revolutionary change, valued professionals left their positions to the detriment of the struggling institution; 14 of 18 Ph.D.s who had taught at UCA had left in protest against the curriculum and the presence of Cuban academics.

Nicaraguan higher education is extremely constrained by its lack of adequate resources – including books, paper, writing materials, etc. – and by poorly trained students who usually work and travel for long periods of time each day. Despite these shortcomings, Father Arguello had been establishing contacts with academics around the world for help in developing his program in international studies. We offered to secure textbooks, maps, U.S. government publications, and funding for a computer. My hope was that North American specialists in international studies would be eager to show solidarity with Nicaraguan colleagues and provide these much needed materials.

After our morning at the university, we drove to the downtown area. Managua is not like any city I have ever visited. After the 1972 earthquake, Anastasio Somoza never rebuilt it; large parts of the metropolitan area are open fields, many with grazing cattle and pigs. Wooden shacks form migrant barrios all around the urban landscape. The area referred to as "downtown" consists of the National Palace, a roofless cathedral, new monuments to fallen founders of the Sandinista Front, and a museum for the great poet Ruben Dario, adjacent to acres of grasslands. In the distance is a symbol of the hold of American imperialism on Nicaraguan society, the Bank of America building, one of the few to withstand the earthquake.

Managua consists of about 800,000 people, 25 percent of the country's population, living in cement homes and wooden shanties; cattle and pigs; a small number of office buildings; the polluted Lake Managua, and an international airport. The streets are filled with cars and buses, with many disabled vehicles along the roadsides. Given the U.S. economic embargo, vehicles cannot be repaired easily, and those that workdischarge thick fumes.

Traveling by bus across town takes at least 1 1/2 hours, because of the shortage of serviceable buses and the extraordinary demand. We took one bus ride and found ourselves ten times more crowded and squeezed than in any bus in Chicago, New York, Boston or San Francisco. Nicaraguans wait politely in lines to board approaching buses, but when the bus halts the shoving match begins. No available inch is left unused in public transportation. We reflected on the need for an expanded and rehabilitated public transportation system, possible only after the war is over.

The square in front of the National Palace is inspiring, with two large portraits on the palace wall: one of Augusto Sandino, and the other of Carlos Fonseca, one of the founders of the FSLN. Across the parking lot from the palace is an eternal flame that commemorates the fallen leader Fonseca, who died at the hands of the National Guard in 1976. Other monuments remind Nicaraguans of their revolutionary history. Across the street from the palace is the elegant Ruben Dario theater, where dramatic performances and musical events take place. It was inspiring to reflect on the fact that just eight years earlier, hundreds of thousands of celebrants of the revolution's success were gathered in this great open piazza.

When we entered the National Palace, we saw two young Mexican artists painting a large mural on the balcony leading to the second floor; the mural celebrated both the Mexican and the Nicaraguan revolutions. These artists and the funds for their efforts came from the international movement in solidarity with the Nicaraguan revolution. Each day we saw other signs of international solidarity: additions to hospitals, contributed vehicles, the construction of recreation facilities, people donating time in professions or on coffee brigades – a variety of projects. Our own country was engaged in an effort to destroy the Nicaraguan revolution, but hundreds of thousands of people from all over the world were doing what they could to rebuild and to help. If more North Americans could see the level of regard and love for the revolution felt by so many, they might rethink their simplistic anti-communist stereotypes of what is going on in Nicaragua.

We had lunch at the Intercontinental Hotel, where we experienced the contradictions that I suppose exist in every Third World country – indeed, everywhere where there are economic exploitation and enormous gaps between rich and poor. As we entered the hotel from the sweltering streets of Managua, we were hit with a rush of cold, air-conditioned air. We walked through a rather plush lobby, passed the duty-free gift shop for tourists and the newsstand where hotel guests could purchase not only *The New York Times* but *The*

Militant, a newspaper of the Socialist Workers Party. Also available were copies of Fidel Castro's speeches, the collected speeches of Sandinista leaders, and other books reflecting Latin American radicalism.

In one of the hotel's two restaurants we ate a big meal – red snapper, buns, potatoes vegetables, and lots and lots of water. This meal turned out to be a rare treat, as we would eat at restaurants and food stands with more modest food on the remainder of our trip.

The Intercontinental Hotel visit was significant for me for two reasons. First, as has been suggested, the hotel offered bourgeois comforts in a society of poverty that has desperate needs to meet. Not until the day before our departure – when we would be in a Managua shopping mall, eat at a pizza parlor and spend time in the frigidly cold office of AeroNica confirming our flight – would we be in environments closer to our own middle-class experiences and starkly different from the lifestyles and opportunities of the workers and peasants of Nicaragua that we had seen. It is because of these creature comforts and luxuries in the middle-class, and the human suffering of the underclasses, that the latter, not the former, form the armies of revolutionaries committed to end the gross disparities in their societies.

Second, I learned that the Intercontinental Hotel was the headquarters for journalists covering the U.S. war on Nicaragua. I did not see the hotel pool, but I had an image of North American reporters covering the contra war and changes in Nicaraguan society from poolside while sipping a cool alcoholic beverage. Sure enough, written on the toilet wall in the hotel was: "Stephen Kinzer you asshole. Why don't you go out in the countryside and see what's really happening in Nicaragua?" Kinzer was the *New York Times* reporter who consistently covered events in Central America from the perspective of the Reagan-Bush administration.

Though the *Times* has a reputation among scholars and journalists as being the U.S. newspaper of record, its coverage of world events is shaped by a distorting Cold War anti-communism and a disdain for popular movements at home or abroad. In the early 1980s, Raymond Bonner began covering the civil war in El Salvador. He did a number of stories for the *Times* while traveling with the FMLN guerrillas, and presented them as real people who had grievances and were motivated by a desire for social change. After Jesse Helms accused Bonner of being pro-communist, he was switched to the business section, and then left the newspaper. He was followed by reporters like Shirley Christian and Kinzer, who manipulated the news to support U.S. foreign policy in the region. (More about the media in Chapter Seven.)

After lunch we went to our first assigned meeting with representatives of the Nicaraguan government. Our meeting was with three young women in their early twenties who administered the regional government in the Managua area, to discuss the special features and problems of that region. Including the city of Managua itself, the region has about 30 percent of the country's population. Since 1979, it has experienced a 7 percent growth rate per annum, adding some 300,000 to 400,000 people. This growth, mainly because of the revolution and the war, has been mostly in the city and has created enormous problems for the region's efforts to meet the needs of the people. (As part of the reforms in the political structure of government, Nicaragua is now divided into nine regions. Three of these, situated in the eastern half of the country, are referred to as special zones because of their unique problems. Underdevelopment is most pronounced there. In the Atlantic coast region, ethnic minorities are to be given considerable autonomy as a result of the new constitution.)

The officials estimated that the city of Managua itself is equipped to provide basic services to a population of about 500,000, but its current population is already 300,000 greater. (Sometimes barrios spring up in a matter of days.) People migrated to the area to seek safety from the war and to find jobs, and the lack of work created tensions within the city and its surroundings. The economic blockade sorely damaged the region's ability to provide adequate health care and transportation facilities, and its capacity to maintain and increase industrial productivity.

Traditionally, the Managua region had been less active and productive in agriculture, so that its population depended on the food-producing capacity of the rest of the country. By 1987, the city was consuming all the food produced in Nicaragua, creating problems of monumental proportions not only for the city but for the regional government and the nation as well.

To cope, the regional government established a set of priorities for resources and action. First, they were trying to encourage agricultural production. They were particularly interested in building cooperatives for cattle raising and for growing food staples, such as rice and beans. They also tried to develop incentives for recent Managua arrivals to migrate to rural areas and resume their traditional agricultural occupations, using their skills to help reduce the region's food dependency.

Second, the region was committed to expanding access to health care, with expansion of regional health centers in municipalities and of health posts in outlying areas, staffed by at least one trained nurse. Health posts would focus on preventive medicine and could refer the serious health problems that could not be treated in the countryside to the municipal centers.

Already in place but in need of more people and resources were the popular health brigades that visited people's homes to discuss with them their health needs and how they could make their environment more healthy. Nicaraguans were being told about the diseases transmitted by flies and why every effort should be made to avoid access of flies to food. Particular programs were targeted in the health-care delivery system to combat infant mortality and to end the preventable communicable diseases that have plagued poor countries. This involved mass inoculations against diseases like polio, which had been nearly eliminated by 1981. (On our travels along the Costa Rican border, we did hear of a case of polio on an agricultural cooperative; the nurse in charge expressed fear that because of the contra war and reduced supplies, the diseases that had been eradicated by 1981 would return.)

A third priority for the region was education, in conformance with the national government policy to bring education to all Nicaraguans, from primary level to adult. In the early 1980s, the government had dramatically reduced illiteracy and had engaged about one million people in a variety of educational programs. However, the war's strain on government resources was reducing its capacity to continue those programs and to move to new levels of educational experience for the people.

A fourth priority had to do with water. I had never realized how precious it was; demand for it far exceeded its availability. Lake Managua was polluted, and other sources of water depended on the rain. In the countryside, they needed wells and pumps to make ground water available. The city of Managua had two waterless days a week to stretch this scarce resource. The regional office had plans to build some 30 wells in the rural areas, but admitted that this would not be adequate for people's needs.

Each regional office not only articulates policies and plans for three or five years, but also seeks to mobilize resources to carry out the programs developed. They negotiate with representatives of mass organizations at local levels concerning programs being developed there.

The mass organizations – local, regional and national – provide a significant forum for democratic participation in policy-making. They include the women's federation (AMNLAE), the Nicaraguan federation of workers (CST), the agricultural workers union (ATC), the ranchers and farmers organization (UNAG), and the local community organizations (CDS). When a project requires coordination and resources that the local community cannot provide, they interact with the regional government, which can facilitate contacts with specific functional branches of government, such as agriculture or health. For many projects the regional office provides funds and other resources, and local groups do the work themselves.

The regional offices also maintain liaison with international sources of aid and support. When a solidarity group in France or the United States expresses an interest in supporting health care, for example, the regional office becomes the center for communication, coordinating the local needs with the resources offered.

Before the presentation by the regional representatives, I had reflected on the enormity of the region's needs, and the depressing level of poverty visible to any observer of Managua's human and physical landscape. But the three officials with whom we had just met had thoroughly uplifted my spirit. They were extraordinary young people. Their knowledge and skills were superb and, even more important, their level of commitment to changing the lives of Nicaraguans was total. They had spirit and enthusiasm, and seemed to be totally selfless.

This office, with significant decision-making power, was staffed by women. Despite the long history of "machismo" in Latin America, these women were important government officials and revolutionaries in Nicaragua. (We would find more traditional role playing in the countryside.)

Our guide, Willie, had some business to attend to in another area of the city, where there was a block-long series of one-story government buildings. While waiting for Willie, we noticed a building that was identified as the office of the government-sponsored Human Rights Commission. Bob and I decided to enter the main office and ask if we could speak with someone about the commission. We were directed to an English-speaking woman of Hispanic background who, we were surprised to discover, was a U.S. citizen. A Princeton graduate, she had decided to give her support to the Nicaraguan revolution, and was one of twenty workers who researched violations of human rights in Nicaragua.

While her main activity involved documenting contra abuses, there were also complaints of violations in Nicaragua – cases in which soldiers had acted contrary to international law with respect to treatment of prisoners of war, and on occasion had done violence against persons alleged to be contra supporters. We were told that the Human Rights Commission was an ombudsman for Nicaraguan citizens and was successful in getting government and military officials to take such charges seriously.

We were fortunate to talk with this human rights official, who was well-grounded in the Nicaraguan experience and at the same time understood the kinds of questions we knowledgeable but inexperienced solidarity workers had. We asked her if the Sandinista-led government remained popular among the people.

Nicaragua, she said, was suffering from the worst economic crisis in the twentieth century. Even if the war were to end soon, Nicaraguans still would suffer severe problems. There were ideological opponents of the government in Managua, and some opponents in rural areas, but the real base of support for the revolution was among the peasantry. She told us of a woman who first had lost her home to contra terror, then had lost her second home and her husband – also to contra terror – but had recently returned for the third time to her plot of land to rebuild her home and farm. To this woman, the contras were criminals and, no matter how difficult the economic situation, she would never countenance a contra-led government in Nicaragua.

The Human Rights Commission was not merely a rubber stamp for the government or the FSLN. Its role was to oversee the treatment of citizens by the military and the police as well as at the hands of the contras. This agency was more interested in serving the people than merely aggrandizing power.

We remarked on the prominent role of women in government. Mainly they were so well represented because so many men were involved in the war, but there was no question that women had been active in the revolution, in the post-revolutionary period of social change, and in the construction of the constitution. In her opinion, when the war ended and the men returned, they would not be able to replace the women who were in positions of influence and power.

Our chance encounter at the human rights office was also significant because it showed us that U.S. citizens have made long-term commitments to the Nicaraguan revolution.

Salvadorans in Nicaragua

Despite their incredible poverty and the war that depletes the country's economy, Nicaraguans have offered solidarity to Salvadorans engaged in a civil war against the militarily dominated, U.S.-backed government of Jose Napoleon Duarte and his successors. This does not mean that the Nicaraguan government has provided arms for the Salvadoran rebels as was claimed by the Reagan Administration. In fact, the United States has never been able to show any evidence of arms transfers from Nicaragua to El Salvador, despite the use of high technology surveillance equipment in the Gulf of Fonseca.

The solidarity that Nicaraguans have offered is a secure place to live for Salvadorans running from the war or wounded in the war. There are 18,000 Salvadorans living in Nicaragua and engaged in a variety of occupations in several cities throughout the country. Since they do not wish to add more demands on an already strained economy, they have sought to develop self-sufficient communities which survive by selected productive activities.

On our fifth day in Managua we were given a tour of three such communities. One was an agricultural cooperative, another a day care center for Salvadoran children, and a third a woodworking cooperative. The agricultural cooperative housed about twenty young Salvadoran males, most of whom had been wounded in the war. They were raising bees, cattle, pigs, and were growing a variety of crops. The land, either in or adjacent to Managua, was donated by some French solidarity workers.

The day care center served about 75 children ranging from one to about nine years of age. Salvadoran women worked at the day care center; the building and equipment were provided by solidarity activists from Europe. The children were grouped by age, had access to savory hot meals, and to nursing care. In the several large rooms, brightly lit and pleasantly decorated, the children seemed happy, healthy, and well cared for.

Finally, we visited the woodworking cooperative, also in Managua. A skilled craftsman was training one apprentice and another worker was preparing small wooden decorative objects. It was hoped that the artistic products produced here could be sold in Europe and North America.

As our guides made clear, Salvadoran refugees were treated better in Nicaragua than in any other country. When one considers the violence and poverty Salvadorans in Honduras experience, and the efforts of the U.S. immigration service to deport Salvadorans now in the United States – plus the underground life they must live while in our country – one has to agree with the claim.

North Americans Living in Nicaragua

There are about 1400 U.S. citizens who live permanently in Nicaragua, including some who work directly for its government, like the human rights worker described earlier. They work in education, construction and engineering. They write for local and international publications. They gather data on contra atrocities for the international media. In general, these solidarity workers apply whatever skills they have to assist the Nicaraguan people in the reconstruction of their own society.

Shortly before we left for Nicaragua, Ben Linder, the U.S. engineer working on water projects in the north of the country, was brutally killed by the contras. It was clear that Linder had been targeted for assassination, like thousands of Nicaraguans and some internationalist teachers and health workers, because of the valuable people-to-people work they were doing. Everywhere we went, we saw men and women from Europe and the United States dedicated to overcoming the effects of the contra war.

North Americans in Nicaragua meet weekly to discuss their activities and what they can do to oppose U.S. foreign policy. Every Thursday morning at 7:30 they demonstrate to protest U.S. policy, with a quiet march in front of the American embassy, speeches by permanent residents, and comments from short-term tourists. Occasionally a performer like Pete Seeger, Holly Near or Ed Asner will appear at these expressions of opposition to the war.

On our first Thursday, Bob, Jan and I arose early and took a bus to the embassy. The bus ride was a bone-crushing experience and we were lucky to get off at the necessary stop. Across the street from the large, white, iron-fenced, walled embassy were some shanties and open fields. Employees arrived in expensive cars and were ushered in through the guarded iron gates. Perched high up on a front wall was a camera that seemed to be filming the protesters. The Nicaraguan police closed the Pan American Highway for the hour of officially authorized protest and stood guard between the protesters and the embassy. Most of us felt that the police were there to give *us* protection rather than to defend the embassy from us.

That day about 75 persons walked in a large circle in front of the embassy. Many had been dropped off from airconditioned tour buses; some, like us, had walked or used public transportation. A large and lovely embroidered cloth sign that addressed the issue of health care and solidarity was carried by one group. The speeches had a decidedly religious flavor. After an hour of marching and listening to the speakers, we dispersed.

I was proud of my fellow citizens – those who had come for a short time to see the new Nicaragua and those who were giving significant amounts of their lives to the Nicaraguan revolution. Over the course of the last three years, thousands of North Americans had made the embassy pilgrimage. We had not stopped the aggression against the Nicaraguan people, but I remain convinced that the level of U.S. militarism in Central America would be even worse if the solidarity movement did not exist.

CHAPTER FOUR

San Rafael del Sur

Various communities in the state of
Indiana, spearheaded by solidarity workers in Fort Wayne, had committed
themselves to raise $32,000 to build an addition to an old and inade-
quate medical clinic in San Rafael del Sur, a city of some 22,000
residents located 75 kilometers southwest of Managua. The clinic
would serve 58 neighboring towns, villages and cooperatives with a
total population of 55,000 persons. Seventy percent of those living in
the city were engaged in agriculture and the remaining 30 percent
worked in three factories.

Our guide, Willie, had organized Indiana/Nicaragua sister state
projects and wanted us to visit San Rafael del Sur to see what the needs
of this community involved. I had brought a check from the Fort Wayne
organizers to present to the chief administrator of the medical clinic as
an installment toward the $32,000 for the clinic.

We were driven to San Rafael del Sur in a government jeep,
escorted by Melba Estrada, one of the directors of the regional office in
Managua. We were met by some ten officials, including the vice mayor,
the administrator of education for the area, two workers from the
union in the sugar refinery in town, an architect for the medical clinic
addition and two administrators from the medical clinic, one of them
the young woman doctor who headed the clinic. We received a two-
hour briefing in the city hall concerning education, health care and
labor issues in the region. Willie and I would return the following week
to meet with workers and the administrator of the formerly Somoza-
owned sugar refinery.

San Rafael del Sur, though a small city, is an important regional
center and therefore has representatives of some ten governmental
organizations, including the ministries of education, health, interior,
agricultural reform, irrigation, energy and social security. Also active
presences in the community are the major national mass organizations –
the Sandinista youth, the ranchers' association and the workers' federation.

There were 15 major agricultural cooperatives in the larger municipal area. (A majority of the region's population engaged in agriculture, but a sizable minority were factory workers). The municipal government included a board representing the mass organizations and the state agencies.

With the help of international solidarity workers, members of mass organizations built a recreation center in the town (the youth organization runs it) and constructed wells throughout the region. The solidarity workers brought not only their skills but also medical supplies for the clinic and money for construction of the recreation center. In San Rafael del Sur, as in many other communities in Nicaragua, social change results from collective efforts that involve local and national government agencies, mass organizations that represent local citizens, and significant inputs of work and resources from internationalists.

Education and health remained the two top priority items for San Rafael del Sur. In each of the 58 communities in the area around the municipality, there were schools servicing 7,000 children from pre-school through high school. They had satellite schools in isolated areas, where only a few grades were taught, and base schools that would provide more schooling to more children. There were 13 such base schools in the region, and one secondary school that had 1,100 students. Because of the shortage of teachers, particularly in the sciences, good students were trained to teach and were appointed as teachers upon graduation.

While the revolution dramatically increased educational opportunities (nationwide, teachers numbered 7,000 in 1979 and 32,000 in 1986; students went from 300,000 to 1.1 million), the problems in the region remained enormous. Access to isolated regions, and facilities for transporting children to nearby schools were limited. Fifty percent of the students in schools had no chairs. Needs were greatest for the very young; 4,500 students were in the first and second grades.

Along with expanding educational facilities for young people, the education ministry and mass organizations were committing themselves to eradicating adult illiteracy in three years. Already, 1800 adults were in literacy programs in the area. As with all phases of education and health care, the central problems were resources and trained personnel.

The director of the medical clinic told us that almost 100 percent of the people in the 58-community municipality had been vaccinated against tuberculosis, diphtheria, tetanus, measles, whooping cough and polio. A Rehydration Unit had been established at the clinic to combat diarrhea, the leading killer of children in Third World countries. The

World Health Organization provided the treatment kits for children victimized by this avoidable disease.

Staff members of the medical clinic travel to the various communities on a regular basis – two visits a day in all but one community. One doctor is assigned to the cement factory and one visits the nickel factory once a week. Half of the medical clinic was built since 1979. Shortly before our visit, doctors and other staff personnel had engaged in a door-to-door campaign to explain measures to prevent diarrhea.

The medical director, a doctor in her mid-twenties, spoke rapidly – making translation difficult – about the enormity of the problems she and her colleagues faced in ministering to the community's health needs. Before 1979, there had been virtually no health care available to the vast majority of people in the area. While the changes had been dramatic, the problems remaining seemed monumental.

Specific health problems resulted from the region's level of underdevelopment. They needed to find a way to dispose of garbage and overcome pollution of their water supply. The river had been polluted by the cement factory, so many more wells had to be dug. Fifty percent of the people living in the area do not have latrines in their homes. During the four months before our visit, available water had become dirty, and the number of cases of diarrhea had begun to rise.

The struggle against these largely man-made problems, after Somoza's impoverishment of the region and in the face of the existing environmental conditions, was being carried out with limited personnel and resources. (Bob had brought a Spanish-language health manual to the clinic; it was treated as a rare treasure.) There were six doctors in the clinic, only two of whom had finished their schooling, so the surrounding area was divided into six regions, with one doctor each. Three of the six zones had been targeted as high priority because of their extreme problems.

The clinic itself was a cement structure with several bare, modestly supplied rooms. Water was scarce – there was none for cleaning walls or floors. A large room with shelving served as pharmacy, but there were few medicines because of the U.S. embargo. There was a laboratory with one microscope and one skilled technician, and a dental office with some equipment and a dental chair. The tiny delivery room was hot. During our visit, about 50 people, mostly women with children, sat in a waiting room or in one of the few examining rooms. The clinic was a very modest structure, with woefully inadequate furnishings, staff, equipment and supplies for the six doctors and other health care professionals to work with. But after I visited a health post on an agricultural cooperative on the Rio San Juan, I realized how privileged the citizens of San Rafael del Sur were to have that clinic as compared to the even more rudimentary facilities along the Costa Rican border. I always had to remind myself that no matter how modest the facilities looked to me, for the Nicaraguan people they were revolutionary advances.

We were all taken with certain patients at the clinic, particularly the thin young mother with a child about six to eight weeks old that had been stricken by diarrhea. She sat at the corner of a long bench with a look of despair and withdrawal as she waited; Nicaraguan parents know what the outcome of a child's diarrhea might be. The health program of the revolution was reducing child mortality rates substantially, so with the clinic, even understaffed and short on resources as it was, it was quite possible that her baby would be saved. Not so before 1979.

The $32,000 Fort Wayne project was designed to add several rooms to the health clinic, primarily for purposes of prenatal and delivery care. The clinic delivery room was abominable, and to avoid diseases, expectant mothers were urged to go to Managua to deliver their babies. Since this was a drain on resources and there was much resistance to such travel, the clinic was trying to make adequate delivery facilities available locally. And they needed other rooms in which mothers who had just delivered babies could have some time to recuperate. Over time the new resources would provide mothers a full range of services, including sex education, birth control, prenatal care and full delivery facilities.

The proposed addition to the clinic required confiscation of some lands owned by a local monastery. The nun in charge was opposed to the construction, and at the time we were there, the placement of the women's wing had not been resolved; later, the nun agreed to the confiscation. What was significant to us was the fact that the government was unwilling to seize the land for the clinic in violation of the nun's wishes. Had the Nicaraguan government conformed to the Reagan-Bush and media stereotypes of it, the monastery would have been closed and the property confiscated.

Worker Organizations in the New Nicaragua

Two representatives of the union at the sugar factory participated in the briefings. The refinery was one of three factories in the city employing 2,100 workers on a full-time basis and 3,000 during the sugar harvest. Under Somoza's rule, the workers told us, the workforce had company unions that were pro-Somocista. Even before the fall of Somoza, the Sandinistas had begun to organize workers in mines, banana companies and sugar refineries to demand authentic, worker-controlled unions. Since the revolution, workers have secured health, disability and other benefits, and union leaders have the authority to represent workers concerning shop-floor demands. Before the revolution, owners could fire workers, with no right of appeal. Now, labor-management relations are governed by contracts, and workers' rights are recognized in both private and public sectors.

The vast majority of organized workers are in unions affiliated with the Sandinista Workers Federation (CST). Agricultural workers are affiliated with the Association of Rural Workers (ATC), and other rural workers and small landowners are in the National Union of Farmers and Ranchers (UNAG). The CST, ATC and UNAG are in sympathy with the revolution and the FSLN but they by no means constitute a rubber stamp for the Sandinista regime; rather, they constitute a vehicle for workers, peasants and small farmers to articulate their views and make demands of the government on a regional and national level. The local union at the sugar refinery we visited was affiliated with the CST, supported the revolution, sacrificed for the defense of the country against the contras, and at the same time represented the interests of workers in the factory and the fields as to wages, benefits and working conditions.

As of 1984, of 260,000 organized workers there were 155,000 affiliated with the CST and ATC, and another 64,000 affiliated with unions of public employees and health workers that supported the regime. There are some small trade union confederations opposed to the government; specifically mentioned was the Confederation of Trade Union Unity (CUS),* formed in 1962 for workers in many Somoza-owned factories and supported by the American Institute for Free Labor Development (AIFLD), an AFL-CIO organization formed to subvert overseas trade union movements.

The refinery union representatives told us that CUS, which in 1984 had a membership of only 1,700 workers, sought to divide the working class and to support the maintenance of capitalism in Nicaragua. CUS leaders urged workers not to serve in the military, to refuse to do volunteer work to increase productivity, not to join military brigades affiliated with factories, and not to join FSLN-supported unions. But the defense of the revolution was the number one priority for Nicaraguan workers. The contra aggression had forestalled advances that would have occurred. Without the war, they suggested, workers would have had more material advances in their lives than in Cuba.

---

*The tiny trade union confederation, CUS, represents less than 2 percent of Nicaraguan workers. However, it has been defined by the AFL-CIO as the authentic labor organization in Nicaragua. CUS has had ties and received funds all the way back to the Somoza period from the AIFLD, a CIA conduit.

Finally, they pointed out that the gains achieved by the Nicaraguan revolution have been products of international solidarity – that the Nicaraguan revolution is a "revolution without walls."

We were invited to return to San Rafael del Sur to meet with other workers and the manager of the sugar factory. As it turned out, only Willie and I did so, as the others were to begin a boat trip to the Rio San Juan on that day.

On our return visit, Willie and I drove through the town of San Rafael del Sur toward the Pacific Ocean, a mere twelve kilometers away. Close to the ocean, we turned along a paved road that led past a large airfield that had accommodated Somoza's private airplanes. Farther on, we came to a town with an enormously wide and long main street. This was the center of the sugar field/factory complex. Along the main road were several structures, including a grocery store and company buildings. Adjacent to the processing plant were the sugar cane fields. Now publically owned, the sugar complex before 1979 had been a vast company town in which all phases of the workers' lives were controlled by Somoza's agents.

We were taken to a building that housed the office of the factory manager and there we were introduced to him and to six union leaders who represented workers in different phases of the sugar production process. In the manager's icy cold air-conditioned office, we talked with these men for some two hours about the factory's history, the participation of workers before and after the revolution, and union politics.

The workers pointed out that the factory, like most in the country, had been owned by Somoza. There had been a union, but obviously it had been a pro-Somoza one. In 1979, the CST was founded nationally by prorevolutionary workers. At this factory the workers formed a new union, but it was not until 1986 that pro-CST workers were elected to leadership positions. The workers had a variety of political tendencies, so the sugar workers union had evolved with the revolution in the country, with support for making their union progressive increasing over time; now, it is affiliated with the CST.

After the revolution, the sugar factory had been confiscated, as were all of the Somoza holdings. Some administrators from the Somoza period had stayed on, but most left, especially those who had been particularly repressive in their dealings with the workers.

Among significant changes at the factory were those involving benefits and worker participation in decision making. Benefits included free health care (a gain for all Nicaraguans), sick leave that pays 60 percent of a stricken worker's salary (the union was negotiating for 100 percent coverage), 100 percent salary for absences due to injuries incurred on the job, factory payments for workers' medicines, access to the company hospital, free schooling, and an active adult education program. The union also gives money for mothers of workers in combat so that they can visit their children. In the planning stage is a child care center for union women (5 percent of the 3,000 workers at peak season are women). Also, the union is pressuring to acquire a state store for food purchases.

The degree of union organization and the functioning plant committees involved significant worker participation that was thoroughly institutionalized. For example, there are three union representatives on an eight-person plant steering committee that meets monthly and discusses all problems in the plant and the adjacent fields.

The factory/field complex comprises 20 sections. Each section elects its own union committee, and at the same time selects officers to serve on a complex-wide coordinating committee that will deal with issues of finance, production, labor affairs, work safety, culture and education, health, sports, and international relations. The most important complexwide union position is that of the general secretary.

Each production unit has its own internal committee, with officers designated as the coordinating committee. Every 15 days, all workers meet with the union leaders in each section and the factory administrators. At these meetings the workers can articulate their grievances; if they cannot be satisfactorily handled at the section level, grievances are raised at higher levels of the organization. Consequently, there is worker input at both section and complex levels. There had been a union contract in force since 1980, but it was when the progressive slate of officers gained full power in the 1986 election that most of these participatory innovations were made. At the time of our visit, the union was in the process of negotiating a new contract. Among the workers' demands were improved transportation to and from work,better education for workers, subsidies for food, and full salary coverage during periods of sick leave.

We asked the union leaders about the prohibition on the right to strike during the state of emergency and the extent to which such prohibitions limit the workers. The union representatives argued that because of the full range of opportunities to participate in decision-making, workers did not need the right to strike. Their grievances could be heard and acted upon without the need for extreme measures. Work stoppages, one union representative said, were contrary to workers' interests, but it was admitted that such actions would be effective if workers were to find corruption in the plant management or the union leadership.

I believe that workers need the right to strike to protect their interests, even in a workers' state, but I can see the necessity for the state-of-emergency restrictions for the duration of the contra war. During World War II, most American workers agreed to a no-strike pledge as long as the United States was fighting fascism. It was believed then that the threat of a fascist victory in Europe and Asia superseded any threat to workers' interests from the large corporations and banks. I would have preferred that our union hosts had defended the state of emergency in such terms rather than argue that the right to strike was not necessary.

Given the dynamism for change from the grassroots in Nicaragua, I am fully confident that workers in CST unions will articulate and defend their interests as they see them for the duration of the contra war and afterwards. They know that such demands will not lead to state repression as in the Somoza period. From what we heard and observed, Nicaragua has as free a trade union movement as can be found in the Western Hemisphere, despite the claims of the Reagan-Bush administrations and certain spokespersons from the AFL–CIO.

At the end of our first day at San Rafael del Sur, we had to wait for a bus from Managua to take us back there for the night, so we spent some time sitting in a park in the center of town. We watched a pig graze peacefully through the park, and watched local citizens return from their jobs. A huge truck-drawn cabin stopped across the street to let workers out. It carried about fifty workers, probably from the sugar refinery. Every available vehicle in Nicaragua was used to transport as many people as possible, day and night.

Most Nicaraguans travel by car or bus, or on the backs of trucks, but that morning I had seen an elderly man riding a donkey. He wore a large hat, what North Americans would call a cowboy hat, and he looked exactly like the photographs one sees of Augusto Sandino.

During the two days we spent in San Rafael del Sur, we were taken to a restaurant just a few blocks from the beach. The days were extraordinarily hot and it was difficult to sit still in the open-air restaurant for long. I would get up and pace along the street to generate a breeze to cool myself off. But the food was good, large whole fish, or pieces of chicken or beef.

When Willie and I visited the sugar refinery, we were treated to lunch by the workers. Several of them wanted to know about North American politics – why the United States was supporting aggression against their country and why North Americans supported Reagan.

I never felt that we were considered a part of the aggression against them. People like the Vietnamese and the Nicaraguans, through their generosity, have distinguished between the official bloody policies of U.S. administrations and those opposed to the policies. Maybe this subtle understanding is coupled with compassion for those like us, whom they see as victims of imperial policies as well. Whatever the cause, this visit to the sugar factory and the meal at the end of our formal visit made up the best day of my two-week stay in Nicaragua. The workers were well-informed about international and national politics, totally dedicated to their revolution and their union, and were warm and friendly hosts.

San Rafael del Sur: facing the camera, two union leaders from the sugar refinery, briefing our group.

A view of Jinotega. The castle-like building is now a health clinic, formerly the home of a wealthy citizen.

Javier, his mother, brother and neighbor children with four North American visitors in Barrio Sandino in Jinotega

CHAPTER FIVE

Jinotega

Before Willie, Rocio, Bob, Jan and I took off on Friday afternoon for Jinotega, in the North known ominously as the war zone, we walked to Managua's Museum of the Revolution, a rather modest building that houses exhibits of photographs and artifacts of Nicaragua's 20th-century history.

There were photographs of Sandino; Carlos Fonseca, the deceased founder of the FSLN; Roberto Lopez, the poet who assassinated the first Somoza; and leading commandantes of the revolutionary struggle; and, of course, photos and documents concerning the Somoza family and the United States presence in the country. I wished I could read Spanish and had hours to go meticulously through the exhibits. The museum did not have the resources to pròduce an exhibit catalog for sale.

After a short visit to the museum, we were introduced to the young businessman who rented cars in Managua, and were taken to his house for lunch. His cook had prepared a nice meal for us and he offered us an "aperitif" and spoke of his college days in the United States.

The juxtaposition of wealth and poverty; security and revolutionary struggle; the lunch and elegant apartment, the "aperitif" and what we would see in Jinotega and later along the Rio San Juan suggested once again the stark contradictions of Nicaraguan history and society. In one tiny country of less than three million people, one group could sip aperitifs whil. others would not have access to water. Progressives around the world have a historic obligation not to be immobilized by guilt but to work with workers and peasants to change these monumental disparities.

Heading for the War Zone

We drove out of Managua along the Pan American Highway, heading north. There was moderate car traffic, and lots of Nicaraguans all along the highway were waiting for rides on buses or trucks and other vehicles that would stop for hitchhikers. As the miles passed, the steamy, polluted city was replaced by lush green countryside. Willie made particular note of banana plants along the way. The flat terrain was slowly replaced by hills, then mountains.

The heat was replaced by fresh cool mountain air. We were leaving the physical security of Managua as far as the contra war was concerned, but we were gaining the immediate comfort of a cool climate high in the Nicaraguan mountains.

By late afternoon we arrived at Selva Negra (Black Forest), a lovely leftover from the Somoza era, where we were to spend one night. The chalet or main lodge had a large dining room overlooking a beautiful pond, and there were a number of small brick cabins set in the woods about a hundred yards away. Willie had planned this stop as a relaxing respite from our travels, the heat and our more modest quarters in Managua. We had a solid steak dinner while discussing the trip to come.

Selva Negra was about ten kilometers north of the city of Matagalpa and thirty kilometers south of Jinotega. Willie had fun describing the war zone; first he assured me that the city of Jinotega, in the province of the same name, was well secured by the Nicaraguan army and that we would not encounter any fighting. But then he mentioned that Jinotega is often the site of funerals for soldiers and other Nicaraguans killed by the contras in the mountains. After assuring me of our personal security, he alluded to the possibility that contras might attack the town. I could not tell whether his alternate assurances and warnings were designed as a prank. Maybe he did not know how easily I got scared. My uptightness was most visible after a busload of Witness for Peace people arrived at the lodge. They seemed to be headed north, too. However, we speculated that they were to travel further north from Jinotega to document contra atrocities in the war zone.

Bob was curious as to why they were able to go deep into the war zone, whereas presumably we would have been stopped. The implication that we might go that far north into the mountains made me nervous. As far as I was concerned, we were headed into enough of a mysterious and dangerous adventure in traveling to Jinotega, and to choose to go beyond that city was the height of folly. In calmer moments, I reflected on the fact that Nicaraguans in this region lived with the insecurity of the contra war on a day-to-day basis and that all Nicaraguans had lived with the prospect of violence all the time during the Somoza years.

After dinner we went to our cabins. Each had a sitting room, a bedroom and a private bath with shower. The comfort was a joy for my bourgeois body and soul. But the cabins were set in the woods in the Nicaraguan mountains. Who could tell how close the contras were? I tried to sleep, but my imagination conjured up incredible things.

Next morning, we rose early and assembled in the lodge for a traditional North American breakfast with toast and eggs. This was the first bread I had noticed outside of the Intercontinental Hotel. We talked more about the day's activities and then loaded our car and headed out to Jinotega. I was sure we would meet the contras later that day.

As we approached Jinotega, we saw more traffic, particularly vehicles heading south. Truckloads of Nicaraguans, some in military uniforms, traveled the main road that day. Also, we saw soldiers marching along the road toward the town. The road was a bustle of activity.

On the outskirts of the city we were stopped by Nicaraguan soldiers. Willie passed them our papers, and after a brief perusal of the documents we were allowed to go on. This was the only time during our stay in Jinotega that we were asked to identify ourselves at all. Five "gringos" in a rented car traveled to within 20 kilometers of the war and no one checked them. The brief paper check had not included even an examination of the automobile trunk. While I admired the openness of the Nicaraguan society, I was appalled by the seeming lack of security. I thought that there must be hundreds of CIA operatives working to destabilize the country in towns and cities like this, their job made easier because of the openness and the lapses in security. Bob, Jan and I agreed that we felt more intimidated by the presence of soldiers and police in Mexico City, where there was no war, than in Nicaragua.

The Women's Conference

We drove through town and parked on one of the main streets. Willie and Rocio went to visit some of Willie's friends; Bob, Jan and I said we would walk around town. We arranged to meet them at a particular store by 11:30 a.m. The women's organization in the area, AMNLAE, and the CST were holding a half-day conference at the local CST headquarters on the status of women in Nicaragua. Willie had been told that we could attend the final plenary session at noon to hear the summary statements from a series of workshops held in the morning.

With our free time we walked around town and found a lovely block-square park where we sat and talked. The town seemed deserted. Only small numbers of people were seen walking in and out of buildings, and only a few stalls to sell vegetables and other items were open. Bob thought Jinotega was very much like a Mexican village, with adobe buildings, gravel streets, tropical vegetation, a cool breeze from the mountain air, and a sparse population. The park seemed so placid, it was hard to imagine that somewhere beyond the mountains surrounding the city brutal fighting was going on. In the midst of the war zone all seemed at peace.

At the appointed time we returned to the store where we were to meet Willie. With him was his dear friend, Javier, who was a war hero of the revolution. Rather than accept a richly deserved high government position after Somoza fell, Javier had returned to his home community to teach woodworking. He was a reservist in the military. He and his wife were separated, but he, unlike most Nicaraguan men in his situation, had custody of their child.

Willie, Javier and the rest of our group walked to the CST headquarters and met more of Willie's friends. Willie had picked coffee with several of the young people we met in Jinotega and they had great admiration for him. Consequently they would give us a warm welcome, organize a big party on our behalf and express their appreciation of our solidarity.

The CST hall had been a dance hall in the Somoza period. A beautiful mural on one wall of the main room depicted women in the Nicaraguan revolution – a series of heads and shoulders of Nicaraguan women with expressions of pride and determination on their faces, painted in rich browns, greens and reds. Across the room was an alcove with round glass windows; its curved wall held paintings of Marx, Engels, Lenin, Sandino and Carlos Fonseca. We were told that Nicaraguans killed at the front are brought back to Jinotega and placed in this alcove during the period of mourning.

In a lecture hall at the back of the building, the plenary session of the women's conference was in progress. A representative from each of four workshops spoke about what each group had discussed. Some fifty people were in attendance, including eight men and five children. Most of the women were young, but there were a few older women as well.

The general thrust of their comments was that while women saw the revolution as central to the improvement of life for all Nicaraguans, there was still much to be done to create social and economic justice for women in Nicaraguan society. Domestic work was never valued, it was claimed. This was particularly relevant in a society in which historically a high percentage of males abandoned their wives and families out of despair or the need to move to available jobs. Even after the revolution with its many changes, women still experienced physical and mental oppression. Social services, while improved, are still inadequate to their needs.

At another workshop, participants had discussed the limited

number of women in high-level government positions. Women were only able to secure roles of secondary importance in the government. This workshop also discussed the maltreatment of women, manifested in wife beating and in the lack of serious regard by the police of such charges. Some of this physical and mental abuse still comes from FSLN members as well as non-party men.

The workshop representative said that women must continue to demand an end to this repression in a variety of ways. Children must be educated to non-sexist values, and young people must educate their parents. Also, women should exercise their new rights to form their own organizations, and – if desired and needed – to live separate from men. They must struggle against "machismo" as they struggle against imperialism.

Another speaker said that FSLN leaders and police should be made to respond seriously to wife-abuse charges. She further raised the problem of child care as a constraint on participation in the movement. There was a need for measures that would afford women the opportunity to be as active as men in the mass organizations.

While the criticisms of sexism in Nicaraguan society were serious, the speakers made it clear that the revolution would be the source of liberation for *all* citizens and must be defended. As one speaker put it, it was because the men were fighting the contras at the front that the women's conference could be held at all. It is most unusual for any society at war to allow mass meetings and public dialogue on issues that could divide the society. Once again, what we saw in Nicaragua exemplified openness and debate, not dictatorship and conformity.

The women's conference was inspiring to us from a number of vantage points. First, the conference participants were men and women, young and old, and they seemed committed to the revolutionary struggle. They could see the need to fight for and defend the revolution even while they criticized it.

Second, the workshop spokespersons, presumably leaders of local mass organizations like the CST or AMNLAE, were militant, articulate and thoroughly committed to fundamental social change. The leadership of the country was in impressive hands. In fact, I was constantly comparing the young revolutionaries who led the government and the mass organizations with the physically bloated, ill-informed, self-seeking politicians in the United States – thinking especially of machine politics in my home town, Chicago.

Third, I saw a concrete manifestation of a principle of revolutionary politics in the twentieth century. Mass organizations of farmers and peasants, workers, students, professionals and women mobilize around issues of relevance to them and relate their concerns to the overall revolutionary process. These groups form institutions before, during and shortly after the armed struggle to gain power, and then – as in Cuba and Nicaragua – continue to act in support of their interests. This institutionalization of class and gender interests serves as a source of support for and pressure on the regime to continue the process of fundamental change.

No such process of institutionalization of demands for change in revolutionary societies is more important than that of the women's organizations. What we saw at the women's conference was a dual, and in some ways contradictory, process: the mobilization of women not only in support of the revolution but also in opposition to the existing manifestations of sexism. The women's movement was one of the most progressive forces in Nicaraguan society and clearly was not going to dissipate with time or with the end of the contra war. Women were vital to the revolutionary struggle, to the struggle against the contras, and to the construction of a new society. The historic force of women power had been unleashed in Nicaragua and could not be contained, not even by FSLN men.

Having seen the vitality of the women's movement in Jinotega and the broad participation of women in institutions of government in Managua (though they were not so visible in the rural cooperatives), one might expect Nicaragua to serve as a constructive example for new societies elsewhere as the processes of change unfold, after the contra war. However, considering some very selective evidence in a few lengthy discussions with Melba Estrada of the Managua regional office, it may be that the ideology of this women's movement is subtly different from North American and European feminism.

Melba Estrada, back in Managua, was offended on more than one occasion when Bob or I mentioned how impressed we were with the representation of women in positions of responsibility. She responded sharply, saying that the revolution is based on the principle that the *best* shall serve in given positions, whether they be men or women. When asked if women would give up their positions in government when the men returned from combat, she reiterated that if the men were more competent, they would have their jobs back; if the women were superior in performance, then they would keep the jobs.

To Melba, who probably did not regard herself as a feminist, the highest priority was the revolution, and she implied that a certain kind of feminism – as reflected in some North American currents – was counterrevolutionary. Melba and the women's conference participants believed that political and economic equality with men could be achieved under socialism, given the appropriate political mobilization of women and supportive men.

These women would probably not subscribe to a particular feminist view, a theory of patriarchy, that capitalism and statism rest on a fundamental kind of oppression derived from the institutionalization of male power and dominance over women, that power and domination themselves are male concepts and their manifestation in revolutionary organizations such as a vanguard political party reinforces women's oppression rather than facilitating its diminution.

These Nicaraguan women would feel more comfortable with a socialist feminist theory that gives priority consideration to class oppression, then incorporates struggle against gender and racial oppression. From our limited contacts with revolutionary women in Nicaragua, I saw their stance as useful for understanding and ending women's oppression. Others may view the Nicaraguan feminism as theoretically backward and attribute that backwardness to the potent sexism of Hispanic societies. But whatever stand one takes on the theoretical question, it is clear that Nicaragua is a laboratory for social experimentation and debate, and that the living history of the country, as the Nicaraguans struggle to change their lives, represents the confluence of theory and practice.

Javier on the Revolution

At lunch, Javier agreed to describe for us some of his experiences as a young fighter for the revolution in the 1970s. As a young student in Masaya in the mid-1970s, Javier became aware of the Sandinista Front when in December 1974 an FSLN unit attacked and held the house of a wealthy colleague of Somoza's, demanding ransom for those inside. After this action, many students began to organize clandestinely.

Javier joined the Student Revolutionary Front in 1976. In this organization, students learned how to act politically and militarily. They would engage in actions, such as occupying a school, to demonstrate their commitment and to build a larger movement. After Pedro Chamorro, editor of *La Prensa,* was killed in January 1978, the militancy of the students – indeed, of the entire society – increased dramatically.

A spirit of insurrection was in the air in 1978, but disagreements on tactics among the leftist opposition hindered speedy development of the revolution. The FSLN was then still a constellation of activists with divergent political analyses of the revolutionary process. For some, the current struggle was part of a long-term peoples' war that might take years to defeat the enemy, like the 100-year war of the Vietnamese against imperialism. For others, revolution was imminent and would occur as a result of insurrection around the country. Opposition leaders also debated the relative revolutionary potential of the peasantry versus the urban working class.

The debates were exacerbated by disagreements among the political parties and the bourgeois opposition to Somoza, which was interested in ousting him but not in building a socialist society. I am sure Javier would agree that it was the activity of the Nicaraguan workers and peasants in 1978 and 1979 that decided the theoretical issues.

In February 1978, after the Chamorro assassination and National Guard attacks on mourners in the town of Masaya, an Indian barrio known as Monimbo rose up in insurrectionary rebellion. After several days of barricades and community struggle against the National Guard, Somoza ordered the full mobilization of arms to crush the rebellion. More than 200 men, women and children were killed.

After the Monimbo insurrection, Javier went to the mountains to get military and political training. Cadres formed in the mountains were prepared to attack key cities in organized offensives against Somoza's troops. In September 1978, insurrection occurred in several cities throughout the country, including Matagalpa, Leon, Esteli, Masaya and Managua. Individual factions of the FSLN dominated certain barrios, and the insurrection was defeated (according to Javier) because of the divisions among the revolutionaries.

During the September insurrection, Javier was responsible for leading an attack on a military base. He found that the people were not prepared to attack, lacking adequate equipment, including bullets.

Javier recalled the revolution as a war of the young. His own father had urged him to stay away from the FSLN, but Javier told him about the long struggle of the Vietnamese to defeat the French and then the North Americans and their local allies in Saigon. His father, however, remained unconvinced – or, more probably – fearful that his son and other sons and daughters would be killed for standing up against the Somoza military machine.

After the revolutionary cadres were defeated in Masaya, Javier and others had to flee as the National Guardsmen swept through the barrios to find Sandinistas. He ran into a Red Cross health station to hide. The guardsmen invaded the Red Cross headquarters and began to search through the building for guerrillas. Javier's life was saved by a nurse who demanded that the guardsmen stop their search. To Javier's surprise, they left, and he then escaped.

When the attack failed, the revolutionary fighters had to find ways to hide their guns. Many hid them behind latrines. Any National Guard discovery of them would have meant a death sentence for one or several persons in the house where they were found.

In the aftermath of the failed insurrection, Javier and many others engaged in self-critical analyses about the abortive effort, meeting in secret in churches around the city. The FSLN factions came together in 1979 as a result of the movement of the people. This showed the lack of dogmatism of the FSLN leadership and the power of linking theory with practice.

In May 1979, the final insurrection began anew and Javier was back in Jinotega serving as a commander of revolutionary forces. He described the battles with Somoza's troops in the region, the death of several commanders, the need for FSLN forces to retreat temporarily, and the bombing campaign of the National Guard to disperse and destroy them. After final victory, Javier chose to stay in Jinotega working as a wood craftsman.

A short, modest and quiet man, Javier had been in the center of revolutionary struggle during the critical years from 1976 to 1979. He had distinguished himself as a fighter, but seemed to show little "machismo." He was now the sole parent of his little girl, lived with his mother and brothers, and did no bragging about his exploits. I am sure his skills as a craftsman were good and his military leadership superb. Yet he was an average person who had been called upon to do history's work. It was thousands of men and women like him who had made the Nicaraguan revolution and were still defending it. It is broad masses of people, great men and women, who make history, not preordained elites.

Our hotel for the night was a two-story structure with individual rooms with toilets. There was no running water, so we had to scoop water from a big bucket for washing, showering and flushing the toilet. Out front, the view was of a small mountain less than a mile away.

Around the corner from the hotel, on a small gravelly street, was an office of Witness for Peace, the religious-based solidarity organization. A small number of North American solidarity workers lived in Jinotega permanently, their main function being on-site documentation of contra acts of terror. Just a short trip into the mountains and they would see evidence of U.S. policy.

When we were settled in our rooms, Javier continued his story-telling until it was time to walk back to the barrio, where Willie's friends were preparing a dinner and party for us. We walked past the hall where the party was to be held but no one was present. We continued to walk into the barrio and stopped at a rudimentary dirt-floored house that was the local bar. There we sat down and ordered beers. Several of Willie's young Nicaraguan friends came by to say hello as the bar filled up.

This was a poor working-class bar and later I would be struck by what seemed to me the differences between those at the bar and those at the party. The people at the bar looked older and more cynical about their lives and the political life of the country, whereas Willie's friends were young, vigorous and revolutionary. But I had no basis for passing judgments about the bar room drinkers, as I did not ask sufficient questions of Willie to justify a comparative analysis.

At about eight p.m. we walked back to where the party was to be held. I half expected the hall to be empty, despite Willie's lavish descriptions of his friends in Jinotega, their militancy and their eagerness to meet us. But we found the place full. There were about 50 people, virtually all men and women in their twenties, and a handful of five-year-olds running about among the tables and dancers. Most of the people were sitting at tables, finishing their meals in the larger of the two rooms.

What did seem clear was the level of revolutionary fervor and enthusiasm. It could be that the informal criteria for being invited to the party had included commitment to the revolution, not just knowing and admiring Willie and caring about the visit of a group of gringos. One clear difference between the bar and the party was that in the bar there had been no women, except the waitresses.

We were ushered into empty seats in the smaller room and several women brought us plates of stew and vegetables and bottles of beer. The Nicaraguans, however, were drinking rum, apparently one of their premier domestically produced products. Somehow they knew that we would not be able to drink the rum. Willie was the one exception. Bob did take some, thinking it was bottled water! I devoured the meal and had some of the beer.

We were invited by very young Nicaraguan women to dance. The music that blasted in the two rooms all night came from a medium-sized "jam box" playing tapes of contemporary rock music. Since Bob and I don't dance, we refused the young women's requests. I had decided that without being impolite, I would not completely bow to local customs, and I just hoped that my decision would not offend my guests. Jan, however, enjoyed dancing and she had various young partners. Willie and Rocio, expert dancers in North American and Latin idioms, also danced the night away.

Generously enough, various members of the party would come to talk to us wallflowers via translation. One of the young women who had asked me to dance was wearing a six-pointed star of David around her neck. I thought it would be quite interesting to report to my family that I had met a Jewish person in Jinotega, so we asked her if she was Jewish. The necklace, however, had no significance other than that the insignia was popular among young people. The young woman said she knew little about Judaism but would be interested to learn more.

Several young men came to talk to us. One, quite drunk and probably no more than eighteen years old, came with a specific request. He asked us to send him a sweatshirt and jogging shoes from the United States. He took paper and pencil and wrote his address and the necessary sizes. As he was writing the instructions, another young man, about twenty-three and also somewhat high, sat down. The second Nicaraguan became incensed that his comrade was asking guests for products from the United States. He took the instruction sheet and ripped it up, to the first young man's glassy-eyed puzzlement. We later found out that the second young man had barely escaped death in combat against contra attacks. His entire military unit had been wiped out. He was one of the few who had survived, in good part because he was a fierce fighter.

A third man visited our table later, a man in his forties or fifties and the only person of that age at the party except for us. He worked down the street and we think he just wandered in to see what the noise was all about. He introduced himself to us, sat down and proceeded to tell us that he had been to Bluefields, one of the major cities on the southern Atlantic Coast. Every few minutes he would repeat "Bluefields," but not much other communication occurred between us. We were beginning to feel that we were attracting all the drunken people in Jinotega when the party drew to a close at eleven p.m.

Several of the party-goers, even some of the men, helped clean up the hall. For many who had attended, it was an end to celebration and security and a resumption of confrontation with death. Most of the young men in Jinotega – most of those in attendance at the party – were in the reserves, and they had been activated to go fight the contras.

The war had heated up because of the U.S. Congress's recent authorization of $100 million in contra aid and the Reagan-Bush administration's orders that the contras move en masse back into Nicaragua from Honduras to achieve some demonstrable combat victories. This meant a dramatic increase in the scale of combat, terror and death. In fact, as we drove to Jinotega, we had heard rumors about a major contra attack against the other northern city in Nicaragua, Esteli.

So these young men, who had been contra targets while picking coffee with Willie in 1985, and had served in the military in 1986 and 1987, were now slated to return to the war any day. So was Javier, who was much older.

The other young men at the party who had not been activated from the reserves were those already on active duty. We were told that several young men had been given weekend passes to come home for the party in our honor.

While Willie and several others were still cleaning the hall, I stepped outside. With Rocio translating, I spoke with a young man who was a communications specialist for the reserve unit. He let us know that he was a Marxist-Leninist and was committed to the Nicaraguan revolution. Why were we in Nicaragua? he asked, with some degree of suspicion. Was it just to see how poor people live? He seemed to be suggesting that we were merely anthropologists from the imperial North or paternalistic do-gooders.

I told him we were international solidarity workers, that our visit would help us oppose U.S. imperialism, particularly its intervention against the Nicaraguan revolution. These *were* the reasons I had come to Nicaragua, but somehow I had an uncomfortably hollow feeling about my explanation. I hoped none of us were in Nicaragua *just* for adventure, or sympathy, or to write about it.

Another young man, the one who had castigated his young comrade for asking us to send jogging shoes, embraced me, proclaiming that he regarded our visit as proof of our revolutionary solidarity and an act of our own courage. He made me feel as if I were a Sandinista fighter against Somoza repression and contra terror. Immediately I felt a wave of guilt for all my mental grumbling about the heat, food, toilets and other discomforts. I much preferred this young man's enthusiasm to the skepticism of the first.

On Sunday morning we were invited to Javier's home in the Barrio Sandino, which rose on an angle up the sides of several hills. Javier's home was one of the many tin-roofed houses in a very poor neighborhood, with a dirt floor and big plastic sheets for room dividers. Across the street from his house was a hill that the group walked up – or, in my case, crawled up.

From the top we could see all across the valley in which Jinotega was situated. It was a beautiful view of mountains, greenery, grazing cattle, rows of buildings in the center of the city, and patches of barrios like Barrio Sandino. The cool breeze, the vista, visions of children running up and down the gravel roads in the barrios, all made the scene so placid and secure. But, as I was forever remembering, the view from the hilltop, like everything else in Nicaragua, was fraught with contradiction. Over the mountains someplace were small bands of contras with orders to terrorize the population and destroy the modest buildings that served the local people.

Before we climbed the hill, we had had a hot breakfast, prepared by Javier's mother. Their resources were clearly strained to serve five of us food and drink, but they were extremely generous and hospitable, like the other Nicaraguan people we met.

One of Javier's brothers had just returned from military duty. He was nineteen years old, was a nurse, and hoped to go to medical school to become a doctor when the war was over. He and Javier showed us the rifles and other military equipment they had in the house. Many Nicaraguans are armed, not only for reserve duty but to defend their barrios and farms if contras should attack. An excellent indicator of the level of support a regime has is its willingness to arm its own population; surely, the Sandinista government would not arm the people if they were sympathetic to the contras.

Willie had brought for Javier's brother a small bag with some toiletries, and a bottle of soap bubbles for Javier's little girl, who was about four years old. These modest gifts were joyfully received. Javier and his daughter began to blow bubbles and this drew the already aroused curiosity of the barrio children. Several of them lined up outside the house to see the gringos, and the bubbles flying about. We went outside along the gravel road, and I was able to get them all – the U.S. group, Javier, his mother and brothers, his daughter and about eight youngsters – to pose for a picture.

Another visitor snapped a picture of Javier and his daughter on the hilltop. It captured beautifully the love of father for daughter, set against a breezy sky. Javier was due for military duty within a matter of days; he, like many of the men in town, was a reservist just called to fight the contras.

Back to Managua

A drive of about three hours returned us from the cool war zone to the more physically secure but steaming hot metropolis. On the way we saw banana plants and passed people standing beside the highway waiting for rides to Managua – that great expanse of fields, shanties and traffic jams in urban air thick with fumes and heat.

We had been introduced several days earlier to a Honduran revolutionary, a middle-aged man in exile in Nicaragua. He had invited us on behalf of an attache to the Cuban embassy to the latter's house for Sunday evening. Since we were all eager to discuss politics with a representative of the Cuban government, we had returned to Managua in plenty of time.

On our way to the Cuban's house we passed the McDonald's near downtown Managua. The Honduran remarked that the food there was not very good but it was fast and cheap. The description matched our own estimates – even in the words we would use – of the various U.S.

fast-food restaurants that provide some 25 percent of our nation's meals. I suppose some things in life transcend ideology, level of development, religiosity and other artifacts of culture and institutions that typically divide people.

Eight people arrived at the Cuban official's comfortable bungalow. We were served drinks and popcorn. Shortly after our arrival, the Honduran who had arranged the party excused himself, indicating that he would return soon. We continued our discussion for a while. Then Willie told us that our host had not expected to serve us dinner. Of course, once food was mentioned we instantly became ravenously hungry, and we decided to invite the Cuban, his friend and her mother (who was also in the house) to dinner. They agreed, and we all set out to find a restaurant.

I could not engage the Cuban in discussion because of the language barrier and unfortunately it seemed to me that the others did not talk about issues of consequence. The evening turned out different than we had expected. No politics, no free meal and interestingly enough, no Honduran friend. He had not returned.

We had experienced a weekend of tremendous contrasts. There had been a night in Selva Negra in relative luxury, and then a women's conference where the participants discussed carrying out some of the most fundamental social changes in Nicaragua. We had partied with young men and women who believed in their revolution and who were being asked again and again to fight to defend it. We had met with Javier, a legendary commandante known for combat, yet a quiet gentle father. We had seen Barrio Sandino and its curious, lively children, a barrio that had lost fifty men and women in the contra war. Now we had returned to the hot overcrowded city and its traffic and restaurants and manners.

CHAPTER SIX

The Rio San Juan

We were not sure we would even get to the Rio San Juan region, but finally we boarded the small airplane that would take us across Lake Nicaragua. Usually travel to the region is by a large flatboat that traverses the length of the lake, from the city of Granada to the town of San Carlos. This boat, with one bathroom and no lights, can hold hundreds of passengers and their hammocks, and takes nineteen hours to reach its destination. Recently, the Dutch government contributed a new boat to Nicaragua, one that cuts six hours from the trip.

The plan had been that Bob, Jan and Rocio would take the new boat on a Monday, and Willie and I would take the plane the following day, giving us time to visit the sugar factory in San Rafael del Sur. But Willie had been misinformed about the schedule for the two boats; when Bob, Jan and Rocio were dropped off in Granada, they discovered that the new one had already left for the Rio San Juan and the old boat was the only one available. After touring the old boat, they decided against nineteen hours on it without adequate supplies, especially for some with weak stomachs. So they hitchhiked back to Managua from Granada. When Willie and I returned from San Rafael del Sur, refreshed and inspired by the workers we had met with, we found the others still in Managua, hot and dispirited.

At this point Willie had to call a variety of authorities, including our potential hosts in the Rio San Juan, to reserve five places on the small shuttle plane that travels back and forth from Managua to San Carlos twice a week. The plane is always crowded and often it takes special pleading to get seats. Willie was told that we should go to the airport Tuesday morning and we would learn at that time whether we would be able to fly to the region.

We were picked up by a government driver and taken to the airport, where we waited in line to purchase our tickets. I must confess I preferred staying in Managua, for reasons of comfort, though I knew the experience of seeing the region would be very important. What calmed my nerves was that our current plan, if we could get on the plane, was to fly to San Carlos, stay in the region until Wednesday afternoon, and return to Managua by boat. Therefore, the physical strains would be over by Thursday, and the remaining days could be spent preparing to return to bourgeois life.

The plane held about 30 passengers; it was small but comfortable. The trip over Lake Nicaragua took about 40 minutes. As we began to descend, we saw nothing but open fields. I thought the airfield was probably just not visible from where I was sitting. We were no more than 100 yards from the ground when surprisingly the plane ascended and circled the landing site. It descended and rose again. Finally, it descended for the third time and landed, but to my shock, there was no airport.

After disembarking, we went to get our luggage from the airplane compartment and walked to the waiting jeep that would take us to our hotel and the city hall. Later, we discovered that the plane had had to descend and ascend to scare away the cow that was on the landing strip and make sure that no other cattle would block the landing. The airport was a cow pasture! Once again events had exceeded my most vivid imagination.

The hotel, one of two in the town, was a two-storied clapboard structure with separate tiny cubicles each of which had a bed, a night stand and a window. Downstairs were two public toilets for men and two for women. There were also shower stalls with big buckets of water in them. A person showering would take a small dipper and pour water over himself or herself.

The people who lived in San Carlos merely walked to the Rio San Juan across from the hotel to do their "showering" and clothes washing. The river was also the town's source of drinking water. In the nearby countryside, Nicaraguans got water from wells, insufficient in number. The water supply was not only inadequate but it was the source of intestinal diseases; the river contained refuse and pollution from boats that traversed it and the adjacent lake.

We reassembled after we had put our luggage in our respective rooms and then walked over to the public building that served as the regional office. It was a three-story building with a variety of offices in which young people were typing, talking on the telephone and doing a variety of desk jobs. We went to a third-floor office and sat by a large table that could accommodate about ten people. The windows were open and a fan attempted to cool the room, to no avail. As the day wore on, each movement brought a flood of perspiration in this hottest of all places we visited.

We were greeted by the assistant mayor and a technical adviser to the region from the president's office. They gave us copies of the schedule for our stay, and we discovered that there were activities arranged for the remainder of Tuesday, for Wednesday and Thursday, and that we were to fly out on Friday morning. We had planned to leave the next day on the infamous boat, but we learned that we had gotten the schedule wrong and the boat was not to arrive until Friday. We were committed to three days in the region.

The only modes of transportation between the Rio San Juan region and Managua are the twice weekly boats and the twice weekly airplanes. There are a few telephone lines from San Carlos to Managua, but more often than not they are blocked, so communications with the capital are fleeting and unusual. There is one land route from the north to the region but that involves riding over some rough roads in the province of Chontales, where Somoza and his friends had owned huge plantations and the contras had pockets of support. Many of the ranch owners and some of their peasant employees were armed friends of the contras; travelers along that highway from the north to San Carlos were sitting ducks. Only fortified trucks traveled the road.

The contras and their allies were continuously blowing up power lines that led to the Rio San Juan. We arrived to find the power still out because of contra attacks. Whatever electricity was in use came from emergency generators, sparingly used.

Later, we would reflect on the impact of the region's isolation on its economic and political development and on the armed struggle against contras attacking from Costa Rica, but that first morning in San Carlos, I was wrapped up in the realization that we were in this isolated outpost of Nicaragua at least until Friday. If the plane did not work or we did not get return tickets, we could easily miss our Saturday return flight back to the United States. I grumbled at the time, but now I see how important an experience the visit to the Rio San Juan region was for my understanding of Nicaragua's needs and priorities.

The Rio San Juan region is named after the river that runs from the Atlantic coast to Lake Nicaragua and essentially divides Nicaragua from Costa Rica. Its area extends from the base of Lake Nicaragua eastward to the Atlantic coast, and it is one of the country's three special zones because of its level of underdevelopment, its traditional isolation from the rest of the country, and its sparse population. The other two special zones cover the remainder of the eastern half of the country, including the Atlantic coast.

From the point at which the Rio San Juan enters Lake Nicaragua to the Pacific coast is about 20 kilometers. When Nicaragua was being considered as a canal site in the nineteenth century, the plan was to have ships follow the Rio San Juan to Lake Nicaragua and to a canal to be constructed on the small stretch of land from the lake to the Pacific. No wonder Nicaragua was so enticing a place for early American capital.

Shortly before I left for Nicaragua, I had met a Fort Wayne, Indiana, activist who argued that U.S. policy toward the country was still motivated by a vision of building a canal across it, particularly since by the turn of the century the Panamanians would gain control of the existing canal. I had never thought of this explanation for U.S. support for the contras, but after having seen the geography and the landscape, the proposition had a great degree of plausibility.

The Rio San Juan is the third largest of the country's nine regions but its population is only 36,000, making it the least dense of the regions. The sandy soil is particularly good for cattle ranching and permanent farming. Of course the climate is tropical, with such burning, humid heat that I was again driven to walk around to generate some kind of breeze. I was more grumpy than usual there, and considerably less efficient in my notetaking as well.

We received a fascinating, detailed and programmatic presentation in the government building from a man who was technical adviser for the Ministry of the President for Special Zones. He was in his early thirties, dedicated, knowledgeable, and serious in demeanor. He probably had a background in economics or public administration. Later, he told us that he had come to support the FSLN as a college student in the late 1970s.

Every zone had resettlement areas where peasants were brought together to develop agricultural communities. Public services such as health care and education could be provided only in such communities. The resettlement policies were established in the early 1980s and many of the communities that had been created in the region had started in 1982 or 1983, with the immediate impetus for their development being the enlarging contra war. Since people in isolated locations could not be protected from contra terror and could not receive the benefits of the revolution, gravel roads to the settlements were constructed to provide for the first time relatively easy access to and from them.

The region had been extremely underdeveloped before the revolution. To the extent that there was any economic interchange between the country as a whole and the Rio San Juan, the latter was a net importer of basic goods. In other words, the economy of the country supported the region; the region was an economic drain on the country. Only cattle production exceeded local consumption. Further, in parts of the region, 96 percent of the population was illiterate, and infant mortality rates were very high. Agricultural workers had no social security and there was no access to sports and cultural life. Twelve to fifteen people lived in each dwelling in the region, with three or four families housed together. Communication with other regions was impossible.

The Somoza legacy here was a sparsely populated region that had had no benefits from the society, a rural people living in extreme poverty. This was the context in which the contra war escalated in the south. Defense and social change required construction of resettlement areas to protect the people while creating a new life for them.

Government advisers, therefore, began to plan for the revitalization of the region, particularly after the contra war escalated. It was decided that agriculture would remain the most important productive component of the region's economy. Cattle raising and the production and processing of wood became high priority items. Resources were also put into the production of palm oil, cocoa, rubber, rice and beans. Plans were put in place to develop a fishing industry, fruit growing and dairy farms. In some cases the basic agricultural activities are to be supported by the construction of factories for basic manufacturing, as for rubber and wood products.

Our speaker presented a series of numbers which were projections of expected and desired productivity targets. I started writing these figures down, but realized I did not know how the figures were derived, so I stopped after 11 million pounds of meat, 17 million liters of milk, 415,000 bags of rice, 19,000 tons of rubber and assorted figures for wood, cocoa, palm oil, avocadoes, tomatoes and yuccas. Obviously, the goal of the revolution was to improve the life of rural people.

Wood processing had increased over the last five years. More land was being given over to growing trees, and the goal was not only to supply the lumber needs of the entire country but to have some for export. Along with the increased wood production, the regional and national governments were giving attention to reforestation, planting 60,000 new trees and recognizing the dangers of unbridled tree cutting. Since returning from Nicaragua, we have read that the Nicaraguan government decided against a contract with a private Costa Rican lumber company to cut down large numbers of trees from the tropical forests along the Rio San Juan. Forgoing short-term and sorely needed foreign exchange, the government chose to respond to the needs of the region's ecology.

Our speaker elaborated on the substantial setbacks the region has suffered because of the contra war, the gains made by the revolution despite the war, and the need to continue allocating resources for defense even though combat in the region had largely ended after major military victories in 1985. Because of the problems of resettlement and contra attacks, cattle production since 1984 had fallen; palm oil and rubber production were cut to zero; and electrical power is periodically cut because of contra attacks on power lines to the north.

Among the gains were nine boats being built in the region and three provided by the Netherlands government, including the large one that carried passengers from Granada to San Carlos. The region purchased twelve buses; in September 1986, air service from Managua to San Carlos was instituted. However, the telephone facilities from the region to elsewhere in the country were antiquated, and service to other regions worked for only two of the last five months.

The regional government, with support from international solidarity workers, had begun constructing health centers for each large community in the region, and work on the renovation of the San Carlos Center was proceeding. These health centers provide emergency services and more extended medical treatment than can be provided at the health posts in the resettlement communities. When we visited the resettlement community La Esparanza, we met a woman who had headache problems, and she was taken in our boat to the San Carlos health center for more advanced diagnosis and care.

Also, through local efforts and international support, the region had made a commitment to vastly improve access to potable water, a dire need in the region. UNICEF had agreed to help construct sixty wells and five aqueducts throughout the region. A Belgian electrician who lived in the region told us that permanent residents inevitably contract intestinal diseases because of the inadequate and unhealthy water supply.

The greatest gain made in the region was in education. In 1979, there was 96 percent illiteracy; by 1986, it had been cut to ten percent. Forty-five new schools have been constructed since 1979. The number of teachers has increased to 400, and they teach some 11,000 students, roughly 35 percent of the region's population. Every community has a program that provides free hot meals for the children.

Here, as in the nation as a whole, all workers are entitled to pensions, sick pay, unemployment support and free health care. The region is also trying to increase cultural, athletic and recreational opportunities. The people of Rio San Juan, in a region of the country that has always been isolated from the mainstream of Nicaraguan life, while suffering underdevelopment, have experienced significant advances since the revolution.

A second speaker, our tour guide, was assistant to the mayor of the region. He welcomed us and presented our three-day schedule. He talked specifically about the positive effects of the 250,000 pounds of material aid received from Indiana several months earlier. Indiana communities had collected clothes, medicine, tools, toys, office supplies and other scarce goods and had them transported via ship to Nicaragua for distribution to the region. Since we were regarded as representatives of the material aid campaign, he felt we should have a report on how the aid was distributed. We welcomed information on the receipt and distribution of the goods, because our ability on our return to document the successful outcome of the material aid campaign would increase the willingness of people back home to participate again.

The aid had been distributed to the rural peasant population, particularly in rural resettlements such as the ones we would be visiting. The assistant mayor said that the regional communities preferred to sell the donated commodities at nominal fees rather than give them away, since if Nicaraguans were given such items they might feel inferior and dependent. So low prices, affordable even for the poor residents of the region, were levied on those commodities put up for distribution, and the funds collected from their sale would be used for community-wide projects such as materials for constructing footbridges or digging wells. In one of the communities we visited, Los Chiles, one million cordobas were raised (probably comparable to at least $250, depending upon when the sales occurred). In the region as a whole, clothing sales yielded in excess of 1.6 million cordobas, and the region had banked 4 million cordobas from general sales for future use.

The sale and distribution of the commodities were carried out by two of the leading mass organizations in the country and the region, the Agricultural Workers Confederation (ATC) and the Association of Farmers and Ranchers (UNAG). Each community had local units of ATC or UNAG with locally elected officers, and regional officers were elected by the communities. Thus, the distribution of material aid from Indiana was handled by institutions well-established in and representative of the communities being served. Our group was convinced that whatever material aid campaigns any state solidarity group in the United States could organize in support of the Nicaraguan people would have enormous positive impact on their lives. I hoped we could communicate this message to solidarity workers when we returned to the United States.

Rural Settlements Along the Rio San Juan

The social and economic policies along the Rio San Juan have been shaped by two critical determinants: first, the historical patterns of poverty, isolation and exploitation that the region experienced; and second, the contra war in the south, which escalated after 1981. The preponderance of combat, it is true, has been in the north, with some contra violence in the center of the country. However, after the Reagan commitment to the contras escalated, a major contra force was established in northern Costa Rica. Despite Costa Rica's historical commitment to abstain from building a large military establishment, U.S. diplomatic and economic pressure forced Costa Ricans to acquiesce in allowing contra units to form in their country. The contra effort was furthered by building landing strips and facilities for training and supplying the contra terrorists on farmland owned by U.S. citizens along the border between Costa Rica and Nicaragua.

Thus began an effort by selected contra factions to open a military offensive in the south to match the efforts in the north. As a result, much suffering, death and destruction were leveled at the Nicaraguans in the Rio San Juan area. The contra war, coupled with the incredible isolation of the people, stimulated the development of a policy of creating rural communities that could not only establish basic physical security for the residents but also begin to provide medical, educational and cultural benefits to the people who had never had them before the revolution. Communities like the two we visited were established in 1982 and 1983; one or two thousand peasants were brought together, given property to farm cooperatively or individually, and were encouraged to participate in the decisions involved.

We were told that in 1985 the Nicaraguan government and the regional authorities decided to launch a major operation against the contras of the south. From January to July 1985, every contra base in southern Nicaragua was destroyed. The army established its presence along the Costa Rican border to block contra efforts to reenter the country, and from then on there had been no attacks by contras on any of the resettlement communities. However, at La Esperanza, one of the two communities we visited, residents reported having seen contras marching south to Costa Rica just east of the community, about four weeks before our visit. It was clear all along that while the contras could not expect to achieve any military successes in the region, they still maintained a position in Costa Rica and probably engaged in occasional sabotage and provisioning of fighters in the center of the country. Because of this, each rural community was obliged to maintain a militia on constant guard. Also, regular Nicaraguan army personnel lined the river, and helicopters overflew the region constantly to observe possible troop movements.

Los Chiles and La Esperanza

After our morning briefing by the technical adviser and the assistant mayor, we were taken to a restaurant that had a view of Lake Nicaragua. We had occasion to eat there twice, and found that the menu consisted of two or three items based upon whatever scarce food commodity was available that day, especially pork or beef. We heard about the backgrounds of the young technical adviser and the assistant mayor. Both had joined the revolution in the late 1970s; clearly they had the skills to be in prestigious positions in Managua rather than stationed in San Carlos. I took their presence here as an indication of the altruistic commitment of youthful supporters of the revolution, stationed where they were needed for the social and economic development of the country.

After our lunch of beefsteak and rice, we reassembled in the government building, to sit in a room on the first floor waiting for the technical adviser and a jeep driver who would take us to one of the two settlements we would visit. The heat in the room and outside was almost unbearable. We looked at the fifty-year-old telephone that had to be cranked to generate the electricity to try to call Managua. The contraption was out of a 1930s movie and constituted the only way to communicate outside the region.

The technical adviser returned with a driver and we all piled into the jeep. Our group consisted of Willie, Rocio, Bob, Jan, the technical adviser, the driver and myself – seven passengers in a jeep whose side windows did not open. I had the misfortune to sit in the middle of the back seat, where one was least likely to receive any modest breeze that might circulate.

I found it disconcerting that the technical adviser was carrying a rifle, much like an M-16. If he had a weapon, there was at least a faint possibility that some enemy was hiding in the forests or along the road and would attack us. Until then I had been under the assumption that there was no longer any danger of contra attack in the South. I had put that fear to rest after we left Jinotega, but here, too, we could experience weapons fire, mined roads or other forms of attack.

There was no indication of recent contra military action in the region but my creative and fertile imagination had been set in motion at the sight of the technical adviser's rifle. What must it be like for Nicaraguans to live with the fear of military attack at any time of day or night? Even if such attacks had not occurred in a long time, they were at least conceivable. Given this constant fear, a ceasefire must feel like a present from heaven to the war-weary people of Nicaragua.

Our jeep ride took about an hour, along a mud road that had recently been carved out of the forest. We passed an area where a crew of workers was using a dirt-digging vehicle to clear and widen a stretch from San Carlos to Los Chiles. We stopped at a small settlement with wooden plank houses organized around a big square plot of grass. Soft drinks were bought for us – the classic and delicious mango drink that the Nicaraguans bottled in any available bottles, including those from Pepsi-Cola and Coca-Cola. I grew compulsively attached to that mango drink; it was refreshing and filling at the same time.

We drove on until we reached the wooden houses with zinc roofs that made up the town of Los Chiles. There were about 2,000 people who lived there. Willie had spent several weeks in 1985 in Los Chiles, helping to construct some of these wooden houses. The people of the community were organized in a variety of agricultural patterns, based upon the desires of the individual members.

Here, as elsewhere in Nicaragua, there were three central forms of rural land ownership. First were state farms, which in most cases were the former holdings of Anastasio Somoza or his close allies. The state sector had shrunk to less than 20 percent of the rural lands because of pressure from peasants and small farmers. Second, there were various kinds of rural cooperatives, involving the banding together of Nicaraguan peasants to seek loans together and/or to produce in common and/or to share the product of their collective labors. Third, there were peasants who have the right to hold land in private. Since 1979, about sixty percent of all rural Nicaraguans have gotten land either as part of a state farm or cooperative, or as individual landholders.

The residents of Los Chiles raised cattle and grew a variety of crops. Cattle, pigs, chickens, dogs and all such animals roamed freely around the land and the mud-floored houses. I had trouble adjusting to this free-wheeling meandering in and out of houses by the vast collection of animals. Where there were gardens, baling wire had to be put up around the crops to protect against the trampling onslaught of the animals.

One of the most visible features of Los Chiles was the amount of educational activity. Partially enclosed buildings (they had roofs but their walls rose only halfway up) had rooms subdivided for a variety of classes.

On the back wall of one large school building was a huge map of the world, painted in bright colors, for the children's geography lessons. Some classrooms were for younger children, others for teenagers, and a few were for adult education. Among the most exciting sights in our travels through rural Nicaragua were those open-air classrooms where adults were learning how to read and write. This, we felt, is what the Nicaraguan revolution meant: a historic process of providing people the means of achieving human dignity.

Past the open grassfields between the houses, the education buildings, and the young people playing baseball, was a modest wooden structure with tin roof that was the health post. Inside it were the health files on all the residents of Los Chiles. A French nun who had lived there for five years spoke to us, in Spanish with a thick French accent, about health care in the community. She pointed out that the war was taking its toll on people's health because of dwindling resources and shortages. Vaccination doses had spoiled because the contras had knocked out power lines in the entire region, and since this happened so frequently, she feared the health post would not have adequate materials to keep the community vaccinated. One case of polio had been noted in recent months. By 1981 the dreaded disease had been eliminated in Nicaragua; she hoped this case did not signal its return.

The health post was staffed by Nicaraguans who had received a few months' training to carry out basic nursing procedures. The post was modest in terms of the training of its personnel, the availability of resources, and the physical facilities in which it was housed. But before the revolution, there had been no health care in this area at all. To have vaccinations, access to rehydration medicines, and transport to San Carlos for serious medical problems constituted significant qualitative improvements in people's lives.

We were then briefed by representatives of the community – leaders of UNAG, ATC and the cooperatives – concerning Los Chiles' priorities over the next year. First, they would complete construction of the center building, where the children would have their daily hot meal. Second, the community had plans to construct a dam to increase access to water. Wells and drinkable water were scarce throughout the region. Third, the representatives told us that they were interested in completing the road, to improve access for big vehicles. Finally, an ongoing priority was defense. Here, and in the other community we visited, residents were required to walk guard duty, day and night, just in case the contras chose to begin their terrorist acts again. This defense readiness took its toll, leaving fewer people available for agriculture, construction and education.

Material resources were extremely scarce. Los Chiles lacked adequate fuel, chain saws to cut trees for housing construction, and supplies for education. All of these shortages resulted from the war, they claimed.

This community had received from Indiana 1,400 pieces of clothing to be distributed among its 250 families. Each family got more than five pieces of clothing. As had been explained to us in the regional office in San Carlos, the items were sold to the residents at very modest rates. The one million cordobas received would be used to purchase zinc roofing, enough for eight or nine new houses. The cordobas raised would also pay transporting the zinc and for the construction labor.

When the presentation was completed, we piled back into our winterized jeep for the hour-long return trip to San Carlos. After we had cleaned up and reassembled, we returned to the restaurant where we had eaten lunch, but it and all the other restaurants were closed; no electricity, because of the ongoing contra destruction of power lines. Parts of the city alternated in their use of an emergency generator, and that night, it was the restaurant area that was out of power. We did, however, find a bar open and it had the mango drink and somewhat stale "donuts." When we asked the proprietor how "good" the donuts were, he said it depended on how hungry we were. Each of us devoured two of them and at least two mango drinks before we headed back to our darkened hotel.

We retired to our clapboard, bare rooms and tried to sleep. I used a towel for a sheet. After a long and restless night, we awoke to beautiful sunrise across the area where the Rio San Juan and Lake Nicaragua meet. While I felt so isolated from my own life experiences in this faraway tropical land, I grew to appreciate the significant character of the experiences I was having here.

After breakfast at a nearby hotel, we assembled for our next trip into the tropical countryside. This time we piled into a motorboat with a driver, the assistant mayor and our five-person touring party for an extraordinary journey eastward along the Rio San Juan. We passed tropical forests with beautiful birds, and occasionally saw another boat; one was a tugboat dragging about ten freshly cut logs.

Periodically our boat crossed the river to pull in at a guard post. There the assistant mayor showed the young Nicaraguan soldiers our papers, and we were then waved on. Sometimes we took some of the soldiers along to the next stop. We speculated that the checkpoints existed for security reasons and also relayed information about our safety as we traveled these potentially troubled waters. Along the Rio San Juan we were only a few miles from Costa Rica and the contra camps that masqueraded as U.S.-owned farms. Helicopters occasionally flew overhead.

Eugene Hasenfus, the CIA employee who flew supplies to contras in Nicaragua, was shot down in 1986 along the Rio San Juan near San Carlos. More than anything else, the Hasenfus capture made clear to Nicaraguans that surveillance was still necessary, even though there had been a pause in the shooting war in the region.

La Esperanza

We arrived at La Esperanza about eleven a.m., walking about one-half mile from the boat up a modest hill to the collection of dirt-floored houses and public buildings. Here, even more than in Los Chiles, farm animals were present inside the buildings. Much of the path we followed to the settlement was under water during the rainy season, so the residents were trying to gather the resources to build a footbridge and path along the higher land to aid in travel during the flood times. We were welcomed by five leaders, representing the rural cooperatives and popular organizations at La Esperanza; among them was a representative of private land owners in the community. They invited us into one of the small public buildings for the customary briefing.

La Esperanza was formed out of seven isolated communities in 1982 in response to the need for protection from the contras. Originally, the people lived in houses that had plastic covering, and it was only after they received government supplies of zinc for roofs and used community labor that the current housing had been constructed. La Esperanza was an agricultural community, raising cattle and pigs and growing rice and corn. There were four cooperatives, and several families who lived on privately owned land.

One cooperative has been organized for the common pursuit of government credit; the three others were full cooperatives – that is, their profits from agricultural production were divided up on the basis of work done in common. One cooperative was totally run by women. It had been formed when several of the men went to fight in the contra war, a few on the side of the contras. (La Esparenza had a number of residents who had formerly been contras and had changed their minds.) Each cooperative had about twenty to thirty member families. In the women's cooperative there were 21 families. Thirty-five families owned their own land.

Of the 1,351 people of La Esperanza, 92 were in the militia. We were shown the perimeter of the community, the ditches dug for protective surveillance of the surrounding countryside (600 meters of ditch had been constructed), and our guides pointed to where contras had been seen one month earlier. It became clear that the constant vigilance needed to protect rural settlements drained community personnel and resources.

They told us frankly how many weapons they had, but said that their primary defense from contra attack was a rapidly dispatched Nicaraguan regular army. At best, the local militia could hold off the contras for only a short time. Radio communication and flares would bring the regular army in. I recalled the ludicrous claims by contra spokesmen that these rural settlements were military outposts of the regular army and consequently legitimate targets under international law. La Esperanza was a community of poor farmers, who, along with struggling against the vicissitudes of nature and their own poverty, were obliged to defend themselves from contra terrorism with the most rudimentary weapons.

La Esperanza was poorer than Los Chiles – it had no electricity, for example – but yet one could see here some benefits of the revolution. There was a health post and a new school with bubbly and curious children bursting from the building to see "the gringos." There was a children's diner to provide one hot meal a day to the many youngsters in the community. Also in school were 61 adults, with 12 trained teachers to instruct both adults and children.

Their needs were like those of Los Chiles. Resources were needed for housing and the construction of wells, and for the construction of the foot bridge along the river. Here – as in Los Chiles, San Rafael del Sur, Jinotega and Managua – were committed Nicaraguans struggling to survive the contra war so that they could continue the social and economic changes they expected from their revolution.

Before we ended our visit to La Esperanza, we were served what was a luxurious lunch by community standards: chicken and rice, and lemonade. We were all served in a tiny house with open passageways. Chickens, pigs and dogs roamed in and out, and one pig slept under the table by my feet. The women who had cooked for us stood watching to see if we were enjoying the meal.

Then we walked the half mile to the river and boarded our motorboat for the trip back to San Carlos. A young woman who had some kind of head injury traveled with us to get treatment at the hospital in San Carlos. Any extra space on a passing motorboat would be used to advantage; they could not afford to waste any resources.

On the return trip I let the spray of water generated by the boat sprinkle across my face, enjoying a refreshing and relaxing respite from walking in the heat and tropical sunshine. We passed the tugboat we had seen pulling logs to market two hours earlier. It was either a very slow boat or it, too, had made stops.

That night we found a restaurant open, as the electric power was working. They had steaks or chicken for us, and we sat in the cool of the night air relaxing. I had showered as soon as we had returned, dousing myself with the water from the plastic scoop, and felt more refreshed than I had in several days.

After dinner we went back to the hotel and sat on the porch looking at the lake. A number of foreigners lived in the hotel, from West Germany, Italy and Belgium. We happened to speak with a young man who had been an unemployed electrician in Belgium and thought he could use his skills constructively in Nicaragua rather than just receiving unemployment insurance at home. He was working on the construction of electrical pumps to provide water from the new wells in the region, and he was living in the hotel and surviving in the Rio San Juan area on $14 a month. He had been hospitalized for a number of intestinal, stomach and kidney problems, but despite the modest living conditions and his health problems from the region's impure drinking water, he – like thousands of other solidarity workers – had committed himself to apply his skills to help the Nicaraguan people.

After breakfast next morning, we had some time to spare before our trip to the gorgeous island called Solentiname, the original home of Nicaragua's most famous poet, the current Minister of Culture, Father Ernesto Cardinal. We roamed the streets of San Carlos in search of the office of AeroNica to confirm our return flight to Managua. I was afraid that Bob, Jan and I would not make the plane the next day and consequently we would be stranded in the region and would miss our flight back to the United States. And if indeed we should be stranded, we would not be able to notify our families of this unexpected turn of events.

It was somewhat calming to find the airline ticket office, pay for our tickets and see the clerk writing our names on some kind of list. We learned the next day in Managua that having one's name on an airline list did not guarantee that one would have a seat on the airplane; passengers were often bumped if others deemed more important needed a flight. In our case, we did have the support of our official hosts, the local political officials in the Rio San Juan.

We returned to the hotel, and at about ten a.m., we were taken to one of the docked motorboats. With the guidance of a young man from the mayor's office and a driver, we headed for Lake Nicaragua – a lake, it was said, in which reside the only freshwater sharks in the world. It was almost two weeks earlier – it seemed like months – that we had taken a more modest boat in northern Lake

Nicaragua to the island party. There we had seen an environment of relative wealth; the Rio San Juan of southern Lake Nicaragua was an environment of underdevelopment.

We rode the waves for about an hour in what seemed a vast expanse of lake, passing tropical birds in flight, small islands with scatterings of peasant housing on them, and sparse peasant housing along the shore. Here we did not stop at checkpoints and I forgot that we were still close to a war. The lake was placid, cool and fresh, and we were headed to an island paradise.

Solentiname Island

We docked at Solentiname Island, a historical landmark for the Nicaraguan people. During the struggle to oust Somoza, Ernesto Cardinal had lived on this island; his lodging was made into a museum dedicated to him and the young men and women of the region who had died in the revolution. The house had paintings of two martyrs of the revolution, among the first killed. In the large main room were samples of local art: paintings, small sculptured birds and other objects. There was also a set of bookshelves with books on Christian theology and others by Marx, Engels and Lenin. This, I thought, reflected the substance of the world view of most Nicaraguans, giving a unique ideological tone to their revolution.

A number of other small, white, wooden buildings were adjacent to the museum, including one where visitors could purchase books of Cardinal's poetry and some of the locally produced artistic creations. All around the houses were trees with rich green leaves; in fenced-in areas, there were a number of cattle. Only several hundred yards away were the gentle waves of Lake Nicaragua.

After touring the museum, we walked towards the northern part of the island, first passing a quaint little white stucco church. Inside the church about twenty children were receiving classroom instruction in phonics. Along the side walls and behind the altar, we saw some of the well-known primitivist art of the Nicaraguan people. There were interesting painted miniature figures of houses, birds, alligators, churches, boats and trees, and a few painted planes dive-bombing the other figures placed below. This was a church of the people, a place of learning, art, spirituality and historical awakening – characteristic of the popular church that emerged out of the revolution.

We then walked farther north and saw a series of small white buildings that served as dormitories and classrooms. Much of the island was given over to an agricultural technological school to service the region. Young Nicaraguans attended school here to learn advanced agricultural techniques so that when they returned to their homes they would farm more effectively. Some would also become advisers to the local government. In the classrooms, teachers provided instruction in seminar format. I peeked into one room and was impressed with the student-teacher dialogue that was going on. I asked our tour guide if there were any particular pedigogical influences on the instruction here and he answered in the negative. What I saw suggested to me that, whether by plan or instinctive development, the students were not experiencing an authoritarian, discipline-oriented, rote-memorization education.

Outside about ten young men were engaged in backbreaking work, cutting grass with machetes – stooping and chopping, stooping and chopping. These young men looked strong and trim, but I thought the work could have been done in one-tenth the time with one reconditioned power lawn mower and half a gallon of gas.

Farther up the island, we came upon some 15 lovely new housing units occupied by families born in the region. These houses had indoor stoves, outdoor cooking facilities, and two or three rooms for sleeping and eating. Newly constructed, they had been built with the assistance of the Italian government, a first step in an enlarged program to provide modern housing. One of our party asked a young woman cooking outside her home how she liked living in this modern house on Solentiname; she said she would prefer to be back in the fields.

We returned to the boat and began a rather bumpy ride to San Carlos, this time riding against the waves. It was really exciting for me, but some members of our group fully expected the boat to overturn. For once, my fears in Nicaragua were muted. I think it was because I was profoundly affected by Sorentiname's beauty, serenity and optimism. Without the war, perhaps all of Nicaragua could some day become like this island paradise.

Late in the afternoon, we had a final meeting at San Carlos with the assistant mayor and regional representatives of UNAG and ATC. They told us more about the region's needs and about programs for increasing agricultural productivity and fulfilling the housing, educational and medical needs of the community. The young men at this meeting seemed informed, committed, and as far as I could tell, appreciative of our interest and modest support.

On behalf of the solidarity community in South Bend, Indiana, Willie signed a contract whereby $32,000 would be provided the region for construction of a large number of housing units for families living along the Rio San Juan. We were shown architectural plans (perhaps the units would look like those we had seen on the island), site locations, and data on the amounts of wood and other materials needed for construction. While the Nicaraguan government and people needed as much support as they could get from internationalists and sympathetic governments, it was they who provided the concepts and the bulk of the skills and labor for each project.

After Willie signed the contract, Bob, Jan and I presented $200 in travelers checks to pay for the construction of the foot bridge at La Esperanza. We had been told while we were there the day before that this amount of money would complete the project, and we had decided to pool our resources and insure its completion before the rainy season. We were given a receipt that indicated what the money would be used for.

Finally, Willie asked me to say something to the Nicaraguans across the table. I thanked them for their hospitality during our three-day visit and said that I was inspired by the level of commitment to the people evidenced by government officials, soldiers and representatives of workers' organizations, and by teachers, health workers and others we had met. I told them that during these two weeks I had learned that the heart and soul of the Nicaraguan revolution were all the committed young men and women working to overcome the war's devastation and to build a society worthy of the suffering Nicaraguan people.

We returned to our hotel, showered and went to dinner. Then we talked on the hotel balcony for a while and retired early. I wanted to sleep soundly and have the next day come quickly, because we would be returning to urban Managua and the day after that we would be flying to Mexico City and maybe back to the United States. I was ready.

There wasn't a chance that our night would be restful. Not only was I wakeful, anticipating morning, but the whole neighborhood behind the hotel was in an uproar. It sounded as if all of the Rio San Juan region was participating in a party. Jam boxes blared rock music and residents danced and sang. I thought the night would never end. However, the next day when we heard that the occasion had been a welcome-home party for some young people just discharged from military service, my anger dissipated. It had been a great day for returning defenders of the revolution.

Bleary-eyed, at six a.m. I packed and dressed in drenched old clothes for the trip home. We found some breakfast and waited anxiously at the hotel for the jeep to take us to the cow-pasture airport. Finally, we managed to arrive at the airport about 45 minutes before take-off. There was a small military guardhouse and an adjacent ticket office; we watched the cows meander across the field and listened for the noise of an approaching plane.

Other passengers began to arrive, and I feared that we would be bumped. Fifteen children about ten years old were dropped off for the flight; they were part of a school trip to Managua. Of the older people who came, one who had arrived fairly early did not get a seat when the plane arrived, and he seemed quite angry when the clerk told him he would not be going to Managua that day.

The landing strip was adjacent to a cattle grazing area and the airport officials had been having ongoing battles with the local farmer, who could not keep his cattle from meandering onto the runway. Shortly before the plane was to arrive from Managua, with cattle roaming across the strip, soldiers stationed at the airfield shot their rifles in the air to scare the cattle away, but did not have much success.

Finally, out of frustration – or perhaps a desire to punish the recalcitrant farmer – a soldier shot one of the cows. Several passengers protested this action. While the young soldiers were in a difficult position, we felt that their action was unfortunate in terms of the image it projected of the Nicaraguan military. Of course, had the cows stayed on the runway, our trip to Managua would have been impossible.

In Managua, Willie was able to negotiate with a cab driver to take us back to our neighborhood. Having showered and washed the damp clothes from the Rio San Juan trip, I felt like a new person – until we learned that our names had been dropped from the AeroNica roster for the flight to Mexico City the next day. It seems we should have reconfirmed that return flight during the time we were in the Rio San Juan. Janet Melvin (Willie's friend, and now ours) had tried to confirm the flight for us by phone, but she was told we were not listed.

Willie agreed to take us to the main office of AeroNica, where we could try to straighten things out. Not at all like the small room in San Carlos, the office was large and airconditioned, in a large shopping mall comparable to the most elegant malls in the United States. There were restaurants and shops clearly catering to the wealthier Nicaraguans.

We took a number at AeroNica and enjoyed the air conditioning. When our number was called, Bob explained that we had tickets for tomorrow's flight but had been dropped from it. Since we had been away in the Rio San Juan, we could not have confirmed our flight earlier; our friend had tried to call to confirm and had been told that we were not listed on the flight register. The ticket agent apologized and expressed regret that the situation could not be rectified, but then she left her desk and went to an office in the back of the building.

She was gone for about ten minutes, and I fantasized about the worst that could happen. In any event, she returned and stamped our tickets – which meant, we were told, that our passenger status had been confirmed. We heaved sighs of relief.

Since Willie had other business to attend to and had taken the rented car, we walked around the mall, bought some soda and sat reading and watching the people go by. Again, the contradiction between where we had been and where we were was incredibly stark. When Willie and Rocio returned, we went for pizza in a restaurant similar to pizza parlors I had visited at home in the U.S. Ultimately, the contradictory history of Nicaragua may best be symbolized by the shopping mall and the school buildings, the health posts and the rural agricultural cooperatives in the Rio San Juan.

Women, children and farm animals at La Esperanza. Rocio is on the left.

CHAPTER SEVEN

Returning Home

Friday afternoon, I was packing in anticipation of our return to the United States on Saturday. A Honduran medical student who lived in the same house as Willie was happy to accept all our leftover medicines and cosmetic items. Since everything – from aspirin to motion-sickness pills to suntan lotion to Band-aids – was scarce in Nicaragua, he could use our leftovers for needy patients.

We also received packages from others to mail on our arrival in the United States. Given the slow to nonexistent international mail service, this is often asked of visitors to Nicaragua.

For our last night in Managua, Willie had arranged dinner at a restaurant where Sandinista officials often meet with guests. Our party of ten included Willie's housemates, and we were to meet an unusual official of the Nicaraguan government, Paul Oquist, economic adviser to President Daniel Ortega. Oquist, a former U.S. citizen, had a Ph.D. in political science from Columbia University, with a specialty in Latin American studies. Years before the Nicaraguan revolution he had joined the Sandinistas, and now he lends his expertise on public policy to the new government.

Paul was an outgoing, warm and curious man who seemed eager to meet with North Americans. He had not been back in the United States for about fifteen years and wanted to learn as much as we could offer him about American political life. He said he was working on a book on U.S. foreign policy. What struck my funnybone was that he sounded more like an American political scientist than a Sandinista revolutionary.

While devouring a fine meal (I had fish cooked in garlic and butter), we listened to Paul's analysis of Nicaragua's economic and political situation. He spoke of a large variety of projects to increase energy resources, explore for oil, increase industrial production, and expand health and educational programs around the country. Unfortunately, these plans had to be put in abeyance because of the contra

81

war. Oquist echoed what we had heard before – that in excess of half the national budget was being spent on defense, a figure that foreclosed many possibilities of development for social and economic change. Oquist underscored the Nicaraguan policy priority; until the contra war ends, he said, Nicaragua can only hope to maintain the gains already achieved in health, education, access to food and other areas. All new programs were on hold.

Paul Oquist's message was probably the most important we could hear as we prepared to return to the United States, for U.S. solidarity workers have an important role to play in ending our government's policy of funding the contras. He was making it crystal clear that the Nicaraguan revolution cannot proceed unless the United States ends its aggression against his adopted country. We were strengthened in our commitment to work toward this end upon our return home.

We left our Managua barrio about 8 a.m. and arrived for processing at the airport at 8:30. We said our good-byes to Willie and Rocio and tried to make it clear to them that this trip had been an extraordinary experience for us, one that would probably never be repeated. And we made plans for a reunion a month later at my house when they would be returning to the United States.

I still worried about our tickets being accepted by AeroNica, but fortunately, we were listed for the flight to San Salvador and Mexico City. At Mexico City we hoped we might get an earlier flight to Chicago than our regularly ticketed flight on Sunday. After all the rushing and my fears about missing the plane, we had some two hours to wait. There was a duty-free store, with expensive items for sale, much as at any other airport. We ate some breakfast and paced until time to board. We flew out of Managua in mid-morning, enjoying the relative luxury of the AeroNica plane. I looked out the window at what seemed such a peaceful pastoral setting of greenery and mountains. We outsiders could fly into the war-torn setting, get information and experience, and fly out again. The least we could do was communicate to others back home what we had seen and why we thought U.S. aggression had to be stopped.

At the San Salvador airport, I took a photograph of the main boarding area, with the bold sign "San Salvador," to convince people that I had been there. About 30 well-dressed, middle-aged women boarded our plane. I surmised that this group was headed for Mexico City to shop. Clearly, they were members of the economic oligarchy that had dominated El Salvador for years. Some were reading Salvadoran newspapers that condemned the latest "terrorist acts" by the FMLN. How strange it was that the state airline of Nicaragua was being used by members of the Salvadoran obligarchy to fly to Mexico to shop. Such are the contradictions of life in the region.

At Mexico City, we raced to the connecting Mexican airline to see if we could get on the immediately departing flight to Chicago. Three seats were still available, so we hurried through customs and boarded the plane just before take-off.

After we caught our breath, I began to look around at the other passengers. I could tell that other American passengers were returning from Acapulco. Some 20 or 30 of them were in a group led by a man I took to be their guide. He was a handsome Mexican, every bit as smooth as the recreational director on the old television show, "Fantasy Island." The woman next to me wore shorts and looked sick; I over-heard her talking about the amount of liquor she had drunk the night before.

Amid this rather boisterous group of Americans recounting their holiday experiences – the food, drinks, sun and purchases – I wished I were back in Nicaragua, not returning to the lifestyle, culture and political consciousness of people who gave little attention to the suffering of the Nicaraguan people and the complicity of the U.S. govern-ment in that suffering. Would I in short order fit back into that lifestyle and state of mind? I hoped to continue under the influence of remem-brances of our trip. Rather than condemn the Acapulco partygoers, I hoped to continue participating in the movement to organize Americans like them to help Nicaraguans have a better life, with opportunities to be as cavalier, playful and self-indulgent on occasion as the U.S. tourists.

We arrived in Chicago with our minds set on a probable confron-tation with U.S. customs at O'Hare airport. Here would be our own struggle with U.S. imperialism as customs officials would harass us, confiscate our notes and threaten our livelihoods for having traveled to "communist" Nicaragua.

Jan was first. The passport official asked her where she had been. When she answered Nicaragua, he asked her if it was dangerous. She said no, and that was the end of the interrogation. I was next; imperialism was waiting for me. The official asked me where I had come from and I told him. He asked if Jan was my wife and I said that she was my friend. End of interrogation number two. I thought as I passed through that surely Bob would bear the full brunt of our trip. Probably he would be arrested and deported. Not a chance. He was cleared faster than I was.

The next stop was at the baggage check. Here, I assumed, the search and interrogation would begin. As we approached the baggage check area, holding the colored passes we had been given, a customs official pointed in the direction of a set of sliding glass doors. Here it comes, brace yourself, I thought, as we headed through the doors.

It took me a minute to understand where we were. We had exited with our luggage to an outer lobby, a large room in which people call cabs, meet relatives and prepare to head into airport traffic. Not only had we not been harassed, threatened or interrogated, but the customs officials had not seen fit to check our luggage for contraband, Sandinista propaganda, drugs or other menacing items. I was positively offended that our mission in support of the Nicaraguan revolution was of no interest to the U.S. government. So much for my sense of our importance.

We soon forgot this "insult," and proceeded to where Bob and Jan's car had been parked. I ate a quick meal, called my wife and then headed home to Indiana.

Sharing Our Experiences

I wondered if I would find my usual life in the lap of middle-class North American luxury repulsive. We were to visit a resort in Michigan for two weeks and I expected things there would so contradict what I had seen that I would have problems readjusting. On the other hand, maybe I would just envelop myself in the luxuries of showers, food, air conditioning and all the rest.

The day after we returned home we visited close friends who were active in solidarity work. In recounting my experiences, I found myself dwelling on the negative aspects of the Nicaraguan landscape, the discomforts of the trip, the level of development in the country and a whole range of other impressions. For reasons I still do not fully understand, at first I chose to discuss my hardships on the trip rather than those of the Nicaraguan people. Maybe I wanted to brag about how many difficulties I could withstand from such travel. I don't know.

However, for the most part I was neither immobilized with guilt nor enraptured about being home, except for being back with my wife and daughter. The issue as I saw it was not that North Americans should feel guilty about the way they live, nor that they should fall prey to the comforts of their lives and withdraw from political action. No, the relevance of our trip to Nicaragua was in terms of how it could be used to continue the struggle against U.S. imperialism. We had no illusions about our individual ability to end the war against the Nicaraguan people, but we were reinforced in our belief that we should continue our work with hundreds of thousands of others. Now we could do so a bit more effectively, with the knowledge and experiences we had received.

We had returned to central Indiana late Saturday night, June 20,

1987. On Monday morning, I called the local newspaper, the *Journal and Courier,* to tell them that we had just returned from Nicaragua and would be glad to talk with a reporter. That same day, Bob and I heard from one – a summer intern – and made arrangements to meet with him.

The young reporter seemed interested and sensitive about my impressions. However, I have learned after many experiences that journalists portray themselves as enthusiastic and sympathetic to any source, for their own purposes, and this attitude often is not reflected in their journalistic product. In fact, more often than not, I have found reflected in the finished story either ignorance or twisting and distortions of things that I have said.*

At any rate, Bob and I met separately with the summer intern. Later, a photographer came, and I was convinced that attaching a head cut of me to the story would add enormous power to the arguments. Bob, too, had his picture taken.

The story appeared as the lead on the front page of the newspaper the next day, pictures and all. One of the virtues of living in a small town is that such activities as visits by local residents to Nicaragua are more unusual than in large cities. We were news in Lafayette, Indiana. In bold type the story said, "Profs Condemn Aid to Contras."

The lead said that two Purdue professors had just returned from Nicaragua with the message: "The Contras are the bad guys, not the good guys." It was administration people who talked like that about who they believed were our friends and enemies; I don't remember talking about "good guys and bad guys" since I was an eight-year-old watching cowboy movies on Saturday afternoons.

The reporter did go on to say that I had seen the enormous damage the contra war had done to the Nicaraguan people, and that Bob and I had pointed out that the contra war was stifling progress in a country that really was becoming more democratic, with public discourse, religious practices and grassroots democracy in evidence. But then the newspaper pointed out that the U.S. had supported Somoza and now supports the contras fighting the "Communist Sandinistas."

The story overemphasized and somewhat distorted Bob's message

---

*Bob and I had a particularly bad experience of this sort one year after our trip. Reporters from the Purdue alumni magazine interviewed us at length about our impressions of Nicaragua. We were fooled into thinking that our views would be presented fairly, along with competing views. But the end product was a whole issue of the magazine with distorted, one-sided articles. My own comments were followed by State Department counter-statements presented to make me seem something of a crackpot. Along with a series of articles by magazine writers about the evils of Nicaragua, there was a lengthy statement by Senator Richard Lugar of Indiana endorsing contra aid. So much for falling prey to seemingly sympathetic reporters.

that there was more openness in the society, given the war, than he had expected. The restrictions on public assembly, travel and political protest that he expected were based on what he had read about U.S. policies during the two world wars, and the story did not clearly indicate this background for his surprise.

The newspaper included comments on the enormous amount of money Nicaragua must spend on the war, on the contras as former Somocistas and on the rural cooperatives' use of scarce resources to defend themselves. The article ended with an expression of our frustration over the failure of the Iran-Contra hearings to uncover the covert, illegal and immoral character of the U.S.-created war, providing instead a forum for contra supporters to make their case again on television.

On the whole, though, our first attempt to communicate to a wider public what we had seen in Nicaragua had had good frontpage coverage and our main message had been clearly communicated: The war was causing enormous suffering for the Nicaraguan people; without that war, Nicaragua could serve its people and create a fully functioning participatory democracy.

Intentionally or perhaps carelessly, there had been some poor use of language, as in the "good guys and bad guys" example. We should not have been shackled with that kind of simplistic sloganeering. The combatants in the Central American struggle – the United States, the contras, the Sandinista-led government, and others represent material interests, political ideologies and structures of power. It is the U.S. administrations, not their critics, that have reduced their policy defenses to simple slogans.

Also, the mere labeling of any group as "Communist Sandinistas" destroys their legitimacy. Having added the political adjective catering to U.S. anti-communism, the paper put Bob and me in the Communist camp, thereby challenging everything we said. Finally, the headline, "Profs Condemn Aid to Contras," *Profs* served to categorize and delegitimize what followed, *profs* being considered liberal malcontents paid with tax dollars to propagandize the youth of America.

On the one hand, we appreciated the coverage and the fact that some of our message had been communicated. On the other hand, the severe distortions by innuendo and labeling reminded us that we must be very careful in getting our message to the media and out to the people. Perhaps smaller meetings with concerned citizens would provide better opportunities to communicate what we had learned and experienced.

We decided to prepare a slide show and offer ourselves to any group that wished to hear and see what we had to present.

Bob, Jan and I selected from all the slides taken by our group those that best represented the people and the countryside, and the changes that had been brought by the revolution to the areas we had visited – Managua, San Rafael del Sur, Jinotega and the Rio San Juan.

We discussed at length the script to accompany the slides. I prepared a short statement about the history of Nicaragua, the civil war, the coming to power of the Sandinista-led revolutionary movement, the gains of the revolution, and the impact of the U.S.-led contra war on the people. Then I would describe the slides of Managua and the trip to Jinotega, Bob would discuss Jinotega and the Rio San Juan; Jan would describe our experiences in San Rafael del Sur and particularly the health clinic we had visited. Finally we would ask our audiences to contribute to the fund being raised for the expansion of the health clinic.

Our first presentation was at a Unitarian Church in Fort Wayne, Indiana, sponsored by the organization already.committed to raising $32,000 to expand the San Rafael del Sur clinic. This group included a Fort Wayne businessman who wanted to do something constructive for the people of Nicaragua, several solidarity workers who had worked on coffee brigades there and a number of people who ran a business that distributed goods produced in the Third World (they were one of only a few distributors of Nicaraguan coffee in the United States).

We appeared first at a sparsely attended press conference, then talked at length for a video the group was preparing, and presented our slides to about 75 people at a dinner meeting at the church. Most people stayed for the entire program and many participated in discussion after the formal presentation. The one critique we received was that our show was too long, running about one and one-half hours. (Each future performance would still be too long, although we did cut back the number of slides and the commentary.)

I found myself talking compulsively about Nicaragua at every opportunity; limiting my remarks in a formal setting was exceedingly difficult. On reflection, I realize that Nicaragua had become a driving passion with me – to get the word out about the importance of the social experiment in that country and to think of ways to oppose contra aid.

It was hard also to talk dispassionately about the Reagan-Bush administration, given my view of U.S. policy toward Nicaragua and the rest of the Third World. Bob, Jan and I felt we should let the slides and our descriptions tell the story of Nicaragua, without using inflammatory language or political formulations about capitalism and imperialism. Given the cultural and ideological baggage that most of us grew up with, it was important to present our case in a way that would not strain our audience's ability to take our images seriously.

At a presentation of the slides at a meeting of the local Amnesty International chapter, two young Nicaraguans and the North American wife of one of them challenged us. They claimed to have served in the Sandinista army and to have seen twelve- and thirteen-year-olds recruited to fight the contras. Bob simply pointed out that all the soldiers we had seen in the countryside, and the reservists we had met in Jinotega, were at least eighteen and many were in their early twenties. We could speak only of our experience and obviously were not in a position to deny someone else's.

They then asked if we had seen the "concentration camps" in which the Miskito Indians had been kept. On impulse I responded, "No. Have you?" Forced to answer no, this undercut the charge they had implied.

I knew that the Nicaraguan government's policy toward the East Coast ethnic groups had been ineffective from 1979 to 1981, and that it had improved markedly since then; the Sandinista leadership was in the process of negotiating partial autonomy for the Miskito Indians at that very time.

Finally, the young woman asked us why our slides showed only poverty in Nicaragua; she said her mother-in-law lived in a lovely neighborhood in Managua, and we should have showed that side of Nicaraguan life. Her stance revealed their social position clearly.

Jan said that obviously they were critics of the government, and that the audience might benefit from hearing their views of the Nicaraguan revolution and government. The three refused to elaborate.

We learned from this experience that we should not shy away from confronting our critics but that our response should be measured, direct and non-confrontational. We also realized that we were most effective when we spoke about our own experiences and did not challenge the experiences of others unless we could marshall compelling evidence with data, reports, scholarly analyses, etc.

After six presentations to interested groups and one to a Purdue University class, Bob and Jan went back to Nicaragua in February 1988. They hoped to prepare a new slide show, drawing upon both trips. As of this writing, however, the Bob, Jan and Harry show has temporarily gone into retirement.

We decided to write a short essay about the trip, hoping to get it published in major American newspapers. I wrote a rough draft of such a column, and then the three of us revised agonizingly, line by line, until we felt it most effectively reflected our collective sentiments. I sent the column to newspapers such as *The New York Times* and the *Christian Science Monitor* but it was rejected.

Without much optimism, we sent the column to the Indianapolis *Star,* a conservative newspaper in the Pulliam chain that crusades for policies such as supporting the contras. After several weeks, we assumed that once again the column had been consigned to the circular file; since the *Star* was rabidly right-wing, we did not even expect a rejection letter.

One night early in December, Bob called me. He and Jan subscribe to the *Star* and there, on the page with letters to the editor and guest editorials, was our column (pp. 90-91).

Though the newspaper favors rightwing Republicanism, it does have a columnist of liberal orientation, who had recently interviewed solidarity workers raising money for the health clinic. Adjacent to our column (reprinted above) was a letter that praised the columnist for that story. Consequently, that day's letters-and-editorial page was dominated by progressive messages about Nicaragua.

However, within a few days they printed a letter about the probable communism of those reporting favorably about Nicaragua. Soon after, the *Star,* without mentioning us by name, printed an editorial that criticized starry-eyed professors, church activists and others who have gone to countries such as the Soviet Union, China, Cuba or Nicaragua and who have been duped by their naivete and the misinformation they were given. The bottom line, the *Star* suggested, had Nicaragua as a communist and totalitarian country despite what the professors claimed to have seen.

Media Distortion

One can know full well that the mass media in the United States are businesses; largely they present the world view of the dominant economic and political interests in the country, and they are critical of government, corporations and banks only when consensus among those interests has broken down, as happened with reference to Vietnam after the Tet offensive in 1968. And one can assume that the major media are not likely to present the Nicaraguan revolution as a heroic struggle against political repression and economic injustice, nor the Sandinista-led government as a great experiment in government and economic planning based upon "the logic of the majority." However, knowing all this, I continued to be outraged by the way the most respectable media outlets in the country presented the Nicaraguan story. I kept wanting to scream, "No, I was there! I saw Nicaragua, and it is not what you say at all."

A visit to a different Nicaragua

By HARRY R. TARG
and ROBERT TECLAW

We are two Indiana professors who recently traveled to Nicaragua. Our motivations for making the trip were complex, but we shared the desire to see for ourselves if there was any truth to the image of Nicaragua that's portrayed by the Reagan administration. What we saw was a society that was so at variance from the imagery of dictatorship and religious persecution promulgated by the Reagan administration and much of the mass media, that we found ourselves repeating over and over again that this surely was not the Nicaragua we had heard so much about.

Everywhere we went we experienced political openness and free dialogue. People spoke openly about their politics just as

Americans would in the United States — the rather wealthy women critical of the Sandinistas at the party we attended; the landlady who said the regular meetings of the neighborhood association were a waste of time because nothing ever got done; the participants at the women's conference who criticized Sandinista men for still being motivated by sexism. All around us was variety and political discussion.

Other indications of the freedom of thought in society were the Nicaraguans' proclamation of their ideas on walls, billboards and murals. Along with the many FSLN endorsements, we saw billboards for many religious groups, political parties and candidates from the 1984 election. Despite the heated political de-

bate, it was clear to us that the Nicaraguan government was enormously popular, and that young men and women were willing to die for their country and the continued right to national self-determination.

CONTRARY TO what the Reagan administration would have us believe, Nicaragua remains today a very religious country. We saw no signs of governmental attempts to limit or prohibit religious practice. In fact, we saw signs of governmental encouragement of religious life. For example, we visited farming cooperatives on the Rio San Juan where the government provided supplies for the construction of housing units and churches. Every cooperative, town and city we visited had at least one active church, and symbols of religious observance were evident everywhere. Clearly religious freedom was an integral part of the developing society.

We were struck by the energy, dedication and concern government officials had for the people. We met several mayors, representatives of regional governments, technical advisers, health care professionals, architects and elected leaders of agricultural cooperatives and labor unions. They were imbued with a commitment to the people that we had seldom witnessed in our communities back home. There was no self-interest in their communities. They received low wages and gained no special privileges beyond the sense of pride resulting from increased rice production or an expanded health clinic.

FINALLY, WE were struck by the tragedy of the American war against the people of Nicaragua.

The war is having an enormous effect on every level of society. Society's commitment to meeting the tremendous need for increased agricultural productivity, continued advances in education and health care and modernized industrial production, transportation and communication are all being hampered by the need to divert resources to the war effort.

Over 50 percent of Nicaragua's budget is being allocated for the war. While the Contras have no chance of winning, they, as with most terrorists, have been able to kill thousands of people and do major damage to the infrastructure of the country.

We noted one tragic example of how the war has affected people's lives along the Rio San Juan near the Costa Rican border. We visited the cooperative of Los Chiles where people had access to a health clinic for the first time. The Contras had repeatedly blown up power lines. At the time we visited Los Chiles, refrigeration was down because of the power outage. As a result, all of the children's vaccines which were stored in the refrigerator were spoiled.

We returned from Nicaragua moved by the people, the difficulty of their lives, and by their attempt to build a better life than they had during the Somoza years. We were inspired by their efforts to create a society based on democracy, a redistribution of resources away from the very few, and the provision of basic needs including better food, health care and education. We returned deeply committed to work with other Americans to insist that their government turn away from the inhumane policies of the past.

Targ is a political science professor and Teclaw is a veterinary medicine professor, both at Purdue University.

Motivated by this outrage and by a desire to begin research on materials relevant to Central America, I began to clip stories on that region from the nation's most prestigious newspaper, *The New York Times*. I thought it would be useful to show the systematic bias of this newspaper that is read not only by New Yorkers but by leading American and foreign scholars and politicians. Other researchers had done similar work, and I thought I could add to our knowledge of media bias by concentrating on the *Times*'s coverage of the Central American peace process during the fall and winter of 1987-88.

During our group's visit to Nicaragua, there was to have been a meeting of the presidents of the five Central American countries. But representatives of the Reagan-Bush administration had been able to pressure the president of El Salvador, Jose Napoleon Duarte, to withdraw, and therefore the meeting had been canceled. This response to U.S. pressure had been expected, as the United States had many times before used the governments of El Salvador and Honduras to veto efforts to secure peace in the region. Since 1983 the Contadora process – the peace effort by Mexico, Panama, Columbia and Venezuela – had been rejected by the United States.

However, to everyone's surprise, the meeting of Central American presidents was rescheduled for early August, about six weeks after our return.

Shortly before that meeting, President Reagan, in collaboration with the Speaker of the House of Representatives, James Wright, had proposed a peace plan of his own for Central America. Along with a cease fire and the withdrawal of all outside forces from the region, when several conditions were met, this plan called for new elections in Nicaragua, an amnesty for all combatants – presumably including Somoza National Guardsmen who had been tried and convicted of crimes during the civil war – and the demobilization of the Nicaraguan army. Essentially, it called for the Sandinista Party to give up power and agree to a process for selecting a new government. This would have required overturning the 1984 election and discarding the constitution so painstakingly written, revised and approved from 1985 to 1987.

But the Central American presidents met in Guatemala and signed the treaty that superceded the Reagan proposal. It embodied the proposals of Oscar Arias, the president of Costa Rica, and called for internal dialogue with unarmed political opponents, amnesty for political prisoners, the creation of national reconciliation commissions, cease-fire agreements, an end to states of emergency, freedom of the press and political participation, elections to a Central American parliament, an end to outside aid to armed rebels, and an end to the use of any territory for armed rebels. It did not, as did the Reagan-Wright plan, challenge the legitimacy of the Nicaraguan government. The Arias Plan was to become effective by November 7, 1987. An International Verification and Followup Commission was to report on compliance with the accords on December 7, and a new summit of presidents in the region would be held on January 7, 1988.

The basic difference between the Reagan-Wright Plan and the Arias Plan involved the continuation of the existing government of Nicaragua. The policy of the Reagan-Bush administration was to do whatever was necessary to destabilize and overthrow the government of Nicaragua, a project that was prefigured in the platform of the Republican Party in 1980 and in policy papers presented to Reagan by the Heritage Foundation. Given the Arias Plan's alternative goal of deescalating violence in the region, the U.S. administration and the Central American presidents had put themselves on a collision course.

Central to the continuation of the Reagan-Bush policy was maintenance of congressional support for the contras in Nicaragua. Therefore the Arias Plan had to be delegitimized in the eyes of the American people. If it could be shown that compliance by the Nicaraguan government with the Arias Plan was not forthcoming, then continuation of contra aid would be justified. By supporting the contras and ordering them to refuse cooperation with the Nicaraguan government, the peace process could be destroyed.

Further, the American people would have to be sold a bill of goods on Central America that demonstrated to them the "democratic" character of the governments of Costa Rica, El Salvador, Guatemala and Honduras, and the dictatorial character of Nicaragua. If the Nicaraguan government and the Salvadoran guerrillas were portrayed as antidemocratic and could be shown to be in noncompliance with the accords, while the "democratic" governments were not challenged, then the peace process would end and Congress could be pressured to resume contra aid.

How had the distinguished and influential *New York Times* presented material on Nicaragua, El Salvador and the peace process? To what extent was it a conduit for the Reagan-Bush administration's version of events in the region? I had read a number of scholarly works – by writers like Noam Chomsky, Michael Parenti, James Aronson and Todd Gitlin – which argued that the mass media organize news materials in such a way as to reinforce the general ideological perspective of the American economic and political system. This would involve their making conscious choices as to what is defined as news, how it is covered, who are their sources of information, what kind of headlines are printed, and the use and positioning of photographic images.

These media tools, the authors suggested, were used to reinforce the general ideology of anti-communism, to support claims for capitalist economics and to oppose grassroots movements representing the poor and dispossessed people. What Todd Gitlin called "media frames" were lenses on events that shaped the way most of us saw the world beyond our immediate experience. Hostility to Nicaragua and to the FMLN-FDR opposition forces in El Salvador would fit the media frame that identified and defines groups seeking social change as procommunist and anti-capitalist.

The first phase of my media project involved an analysis of three months of *New York Times* coverage of the Central American peace process, from August 1987, when the accord was signed, to November 1987, when it was to take effect. During that period, there were 177 stories in the newspaper on Central America and the peace process, on political strife within individual affected nations, on a variety of opposition political movements, and covering the ongoing debates within the United States concerning the plan and continued U.S. assistance to the Nicaraguan Contras.

Of the 177 stories, about 55 percent dealt with Nicaragua. This was extraordinarily disproportionate coverage; 16 percent dealt with El Salvador, and only one percent with Honduras and Guatemala. Despite the fact that the peace process was to encompass all five signatory countries, that there was a major civil war raging in El Salvador, and that U.S. troops and bases dotted the Honduran countryside, the newspaper presented the problems of Central America – as did Reagan and Bush – as depending entirely on Nicaragua.

Among the articles were 141 statements about compliance with the treaty. Of these, 17 percent dealt with Nicaraguan noncompliance; statements about Honduran noncompliance constituted only 2 percent, and about El Salvador, one percent. If some reports chronicled moves by the Nicaraguan government to comply with the accords, they would be accompanied by comments to suggest that these moves were merely cosmetic.

This emphasis in the stories served to distort the significant moves made by the Nicaraguan government to comply with the letter and spirit of the treaty – creating a national commission for reconciliation, reiterating its program of amnesty for contra fighters and reopening the offices of *La Prensa*. President Duarte of El Salvador planned a dialogue with the guerrilla opposition, but it was cut short in October by the assassination by death squads of Herbert Anaya, president of the non-governmental Salvadoran Human Rights Commission and by the general increase in assassinations and political repression. Honduran leaders went so far in their non-compliance as to deny the existence of any repressed political opposition in their country – further, to deny that any contras resided in Honduras.

Many *New York Times* articles made evaluative references to countries in the region – some overt, some subtle. Of some 163 references to Nicaragua and El Salvador, 61 percent were negative about Nicaragua and only 13 percent positive; about El Salvador 9 percent were positive and 9 percent negative. There were 35 stories that dealt with government acts of political repression and the death squads. Sixty-six percent dealt with Nicaraguan repression, 29 percent were about El Salvador, and 6 percent about Honduras.

Seventy-nine percent of the stories that mentioned forces in opposition to the Central American governments were about opposition to the government of Nicaragua; only 12 percent had anything to do with the opposition in El Salvador. Comparing stories with evaluative references to the Nicaraguan contras and the opposition FMLN–FDR in El Salvador, 22 percent of references to the contras were positive and 13 percent negative. References to the Salvadoran guerrilla opposition were 3 percent positive and 68 percent negative.

What all these numbers added up to was a *New York Times* portrait of Nicaragua as the major violator of the peace process and democracy in the region. According to the *Times,* the Nicaraguan government was not in full compliance with the treaty and to the extent that it did comply, it was a trick – the Nicaraguan government was bad and engaged in the bulk of the repression in the region. The paper's stories emphasized the internal and external opposition to Nicaragua's government, picturing it as more significant than the opposition to the Salvadoran government. Finally, the FMLN–FDR of El Salvador was presented by the *Times* as a considerably more violent, terrorist organization than the contras.

For example, James Le Moyne, on August 10, 1987, just after the treaty's endorsement by the Central American presidents, wrote that the newly signed treaty "fail[ed] to address some of the region's most difficult problems," but it could develop a positive momentum. He reported that Costa Rican and Nicaraguan officials were optimistic about its success but Salvadoran and Honduran officials "as well as diplomats from outside the region" were less optimistic. The number one problem, he said, was the ongoing conflict between "the United States-backed rebels against the Soviet-supported Sandinista Government of Nicaragua." Clearly, for him the important context was the East-West struggle.

He wrote of other conflicts, including the "leftist insurgencies in El Salvador and Guatemala." Of secondary importance was the Salvadoran civil war, which has taken more than 70,000 lives and in which the

United States has invested more than $3 billion bolstering the Salvadoran government's counterinsurgency program. LeMoyne made explicit the priority that would characterize the *Times*'s coverage in the future: "The new treaty is regional in scope, but there is no doubt that its main provisions are principally directed at Nicaragua and will affect Nicaragua more than any of the other nations that signed the accord." But the treaty's provisions to end all support for outside military intervention in the region were directed equally at Honduras and El Salvador, not only at Nicaragua.

Le Moyne's emphasis minimized the regional aspect and his caricature of the Nicaraguan government was also stated clearly: "In essence the treaty guarantees political survival to the Sandinistas if they agree to stop running the country like a one-party revolutionary socialist state." No qualifying mention by him of the 1984 elections in Nicaragua, the multiparty parliament, the popular organizations, the clear openness of political space existing in the country despite the war, or of the fact that whatever restraints on political freedom have been applied have been related to the total war situation.

Of course, LeMoyne did not explain how he could call a country "socialist" in which 60 percent of the economy is in the hands of the private sector. He wrote that "one diplomat said" the impact of the treaty would be to change the Nicaraguan government from a "home-grown form of Cuban-style Marxism" to a "Mexican one-party state" with vocal opposition. Presumably for LeMoyne that would be better than what exists now.

While the peace plan was for LeMoyne a document directed toward Nicaragua's democratization, it did not go as far toward this end as was wanted by Reagan and Bush. Ultimately it will not "threaten their strong hold on power after eight years of domination." The Sandinista government is portrayed as an alien force that has imposed itself on the Nicaraguan people, again a portrait that contradicts historical reality but fits closely the Reagan-Bush administration lens on the country. LeMoyne went on to suggest that even if democracy were to appear in Nicaragua, opponents of the regime would not be very successful; not because they would be unpopular but because "the political opposition is badly divided and weakened by years of police harassment, powerlessness and the departure into exile of hundreds of thousands of opponents of the Sandinistas."

Despite all the weaknesses of the treaty as it applies to Nicaragua, its application would bring about change. " . . . [I]f the Sandinistas genuinely permit restoration of a free press, free organization of political parties and political rallies, as well as a return of exiles and rebels seeking amnesty, they will have made a major shift in the way they exercise their power." Of course, a reading of recent history not constrained by the LeMoyne/*New York Times*/Reagan-Bush frame would make plain that political parties, political rallies, an amnesty program and relatively free elections already existed in Nicaragua. Their censorship of the press can be understood as part of the state of emergency and the war the nation faced.

Stephen Kinzer wrote a story (October 24, 1987) that attempted to prove the contra claim that they were a significant military force in Nicaragua. He wrote that "the Contras have been building their strength in Central Nicaragua, and are apparently seeking to demonstrate their power as the Central American peace process advances." A contra spokesman was quoted as indicating that his movement is strong and must be taken seriously in any negotiations.

It could be added that demonstrated military prowess would strengthen the Reagan-Bush administration's requests to Congress for more contra aid. Kinzer wrote of a specific series of attacks in the province of Chontales to demonstrate the contra claim. A village mayor was quoted: "We see they aren't as weak as we thought they were." Kinzer's report included contra claims that they had burned 18 military trucks. But it also suggested that despite their growing presence, influence and military power, the contras' military equipment was no match for the government forces. "The Sandinista army heavily outnumbers the contras. In addition, the Sandinistas have trucks and jeeps while the contras move on foot."

In the next day's story, Kinzer reminded his readers that the Nicaraguan government had not made "broad new concessions" to the Church, such as lifting a ban on 18 exiled priests and Church news radio programs. No further description of the nature of their demands appeared in the story.

Also, demands for amnesty were not being met. "At the bishops' headquarters in Managua, a new pile of mail arrives each day consisting mainly of letters from relatives of prisoners." The story indicated that the Nicaraguan government considered many of those for whom release was sought as guilty of crimes during service in Somoza's National Guard or as saboteurs in support of the contras. The Church, he said, was pleading for the release of all but common criminals to reduce the polarization in the society. No credence was given in the story to the government's commitment to punish those who had committed crimes against the population.

Repeatedly the newspaper ran stories that presented contra charges or charges by the president of El Salvador or claims made by the U.S. government with very little by way of rebuttal. If a rebuttal did appear, it was usually from an official Nicaraguan government source and, hence, portrayed as not legitimate. A James LeMoyne story (October 30, 1987) noted in the lead that the "top exiled political leaders of the Miskito Indians and other indigenous peoples of Nicaragua asserted today that the Nicaraguan government had reneged on a promise to begin peace talks with Indian rebel officials." Brooklyn Rivera, one of the pro-contra Miskito leaders, was cited as complaining about an offer to negotiate in Managua that had been canceled by the government. The Nicaraguan government's conditions for beginning talks were considered "unacceptable" by the Miskito leaders because they were asked to accept amnesty to be invited to Managua.

As for the past history of conflict between Managua and the Atlantic Coast peoples, this was the background provided by LeMoyne: "In 1981 and 1982, the Sandinistas shot several Indians, burned a number of their villages, imprisoned their leaders and forced thousands of Indians into government camps. More than 12,000 Indians fled to Honduras." Not discussed was the history of relations between Managua and the Atlantic Coast peoples both before and after the revolution, and not reported was the fact that the Sandinista government had admitted errors in its policy and was in the process of establishing regional autonomy for the Atlantic Coast; thus the reader was left with a portrait of a bloodthirsty Sandinista army bent on slaughter of victimized peoples.

Finally, shortly before the accords were to take effect, with President Reagan talking again about an aid package for the contras, Lindsey Gruson's story on November 5 was headlined "For Contras in One Area, Growing Civilian Support." Of a trip arranged specifically for reporters, Gruson wrote of having seen what no other mainstream journalist on the trip claimed: "In a 48-hour trip over three days with a contra patrol in North-Central Nicaragua that began last weekend, reporters found that the rebels were exploiting such popular discontent to build what amounts to an underground civilian wing of the guerrilla movement."

For Gruson, the level of contra support "contradicted the Sandinista argument that the contras are little more than an unpopular appendage of the Reagan Administration, relying on American financial and military support to survive." The guerrillas had begun to make the transition to "the politically astute, self-sufficient guerrilla army they must become if they are to cut the long odds against their struggle to overthrow the Sandinista government."

Some of Gruson's text was convoluted and unclear. For example, "Western and Latin diplomats say the contras' political success has combined with rising popular discontent to give the rebels a semi-permanent base in, if not control of, many rural, traditionally independent areas in the highlands." Can they have a "semi-permanent base" in an area and not control it? A "Latin military specialist" said: "The Sandinistas don't go in, so the Contras dominate, even if they don't control." How can they dominate and not control?

Gruson quoted a claim from "diplomats" that 60 percent of the country was contested, but admitted, "The Government maintains tight control of all major population centers and the vital transportation routes."

In sum, the portrait by *The New York Times* of Central America and the peace process drawn conformed to that presented by the Reagan-Bush administration, opposing the peace process, resenting the obstruction it presented for continued contra aid and seeing its success as placing limits on U.S. influence in the region. The newspaper's coverage was profoundly anti-Sandinista, anti-change, pro-contra and supportive of the repressive Honduran and Salvadoran governments. The thousands of Central American solidarity workers who opposed contra aid, military aid to the government of El Salvador and the militarization of Honduras had to struggle against this attempt to control the minds of our fellow Americans by the powerful mass media organizations. Despite their power, many polls repeatedly indicated that we were still winning the battle for people's minds. We just could not lessen our efforts.

After World War II, when countries that had been colonies gained their independence it was assumed that they would then be able to establish economic and political systems of their own choice. But, as the years wore on, progressive peoples around the world began to talk about neocolonialism, a condition of economic and political dependency on the servitude to the core capitalist powers, despite formal independence. Neo-colonialism had long been the condition of Latin American countries; most of them had been independent from Spain since the 1820s.

Neocolonialism was aided by the ruling class in the dependent country. Indigenous elites in neocolonial countries owned and controlled the land, the means of production, the industries and businesses along with the foreign superpower's ruling class. These indigenous elites were beneficiaries of the system of exploitation imposed by the international capitalist system.

Neocolonialism prospered, utilizing the enormous pool of cheap labor in dependent countries. Peasants produced the basic goods in demand in the industrialized world. With the application of agricultural technologies, peasant farmers were forced off the land they had owned or worked for centuries and became agricultural workers on large plantations and farms.

This displacement of peasants, no longer able to grow enough to sustain themselves, created a pool of cheap labor that could be forced or enticed to work in factories that increasingly dotted the Third World landscape. Over the last forty years, foreign capital flowed in ever increasing amounts to these countries. Indigenous ruling classes became junior partners in the worldwide mobility of capital, while an exploited industrial working class joined the marginalized peasants at the base of these societies.

Neocolonialism is not a stable system. Despite the poverty, ill-health, illiteracy and powerlessness they share, Third World peoples become conscious of their collective plight and its structural causes, sometimes prodded by politically active minorities. Reform and revolutionary movements form seeking to oust those ruling elites who control the economic and political processes for their own benefit and that of international capitalism. Middle-class people and social institutions, sometimes benefitting and sometimes victimized by neocolonialism, are forced to take a stand on the side of order or of change as polarization in the society proceeds. In Latin America, the Church is an institution that in recent years has tilted toward the poor and powerless, giving legitimacy to movements for fundamental change.

Neocolonialism is also a system of institutionalized violence, of expropriation of the products of the labor of workers and peasants for the benefit of indigenous ruling classes and their foreign partners. The structural causes of poverty in people's lives are masked by religiosity, patriotism, warnings of the dangers of communism, or other forms of obfuscation. However, given the stark nakedness of the exploitation, such efforts do not long sustain the system. Hence, direct violence against the people follows as a regular feature of neocolonialism, as the local ruling classes that control the state and the military seek to crush popular resistance, their efforts supported by the dominating great powers.

There has been no precise formula for liberation movements, and in each case the goal has been to break the neocolonialist lines between the core capitalist country and the dependent one. A critical factor in establishing independence is the ouster of the indigenous ruling classes from control of the state and military apparatus; there must cease to be a class whose reason for being is the exploitation of its country's own people. The new state that results can then, based upon political and economic self-determination, reestablish relations with the core capitalist state and others. Ending neocolonialism does not require a complete break with the former neocolonial power, but rather a reconstitution of that relationship on the basis of equity.

Internally, liberation from neocolonialism is a process of creating an equitable economic and political system whose fundamental attribute is commitment to the health and wellbeing of the population at large. Improved health and education, greater access to housing, water and food, and the capacity to participate in the political life of the country become top priorities of the new regime.

While each country has its own history, Nicaragua's fits the pattern of neocolonialism described above. The Somoza dynasty was put in power by the United States, and it then established economic and political control over the country's peasants and workers. They organized in a variety of ways to overthrow the neocolonialist power and began the long struggle to reconstitute an autonomous economic and political system that the United States and those Nicaraguans who were beneficiaries of the old system seek to destroy.

From the standpoint of U.S. interests, the Nicaraguan challenge to the whole system of neocolonialism constitutes more of a threat than any specific changes in U.S. investment opportunities in that country. Thus, U.S. policy has been one of sustained hostility, seeking to prove by the Nicaraguan example that people cannot liberate themselves from neocolonialism; the Nicaraguan revolution, by virtue of its very existence, is trying to prove that such liberation *is* possible.

On our brief trip across Nicaragua we saw evidences everywhere of liberation in process: attempts to expand education at the university; serious debate on the oppression of women; the struggle against all odds to improve health care; the building of agricultural cooperatives, the construction of housing and recreational units, and the defense of the country. It is an exhilarating and at the same time a dangerous process for the Nicaraguan people. Exhilarating, because it mobilizes them to participate in their own future in a way they had never experienced before throughout their history. Dangerous, because the U.S.-backed contras have targeted for assassination those people working to change their lives.

We felt we got to know a little better what the United States was fighting against, and we have tried to tell that story. The end result of the efforts of the thousands of North Americans like us should be to build a political movement in this country committed to ending U.S. interventionism in Central America *and* to building solidarity with the peoples of Central America. Organizing against interventionism means opposing contra aid, saying no to billions of dollars in aid to El Salvador, no to the militarization of Honduras, to military aid to Guatemala, and to the efforts to pressure Costa Rica to act more in concert with U.S. interests. In solidarity with the peoples of Central America, we raise money to support their cause, use whatever talents we have to help them with technical assistance, and defend them within our own country against the distortions of the mass media.

We do all this knowing that, to some extent, their struggle for liberation is our own. To the extent that we successfully build an anti-interventionary movement in solidarity with the peoples of Central America, we are that much closer to building a movement for the liberation of the peoples of the United States. And that, after all, is the long-term task.

A briefing by leaders of local popular organizations in La Esperanza.
Willie is at left.

CHAPTER EIGHT

From 1987 to the 10th Anniversary of the Nicaraguan Revolution

Our visit to Nicaragua came at a critical juncture in the country's struggle for revolutionary change. We witnessed the spirit of the revolution, youthful commitment to the revolutionary process, and a government and party, committed to improving the quality of people's lives in a society in which ten years ago only the wealthy few had lived comfortably. We also saw seeds being planted for a survival society, one in which future gains would have to be postponed and resources invested in preserving what had already been achieved. In brief, revolutionary change was being transformed into maintaining the status quo.

We were in Nicaragua during a time when fierce fighting, death and destruction were characteristic features of the contra war, but our visit also coincided with the beginning of the end for the contras. In the several months after our return to the United States, their fighting capability was dramatically destroyed.

Further, our visit occurred at a time when the military struggle of the Nicaraguan people against imperialism was being transformed to a diplomatic one. Shortly after our return to the United States, the Central American presidents met at Esquipulas, near Guatemala City, and signed the Central American Peace Treaty. From that point on, the Nicaraguan government intensified its efforts in diplomatic conference rooms and with the world's media. Thus our short stay occurred when the swirl of events was transforming Central America in ways we would not have predicted.

Just two years after our trip, many elements of the political and economic landscape have changed significantly in the region, in the tactics of U.S. foreign policy and in the character of the struggles for progressive change in Nicaragua. Most importantly, the Reagan administration, with its murderous policy of extermination of

Central American peoples, is gone, while the revolution in Nicaragua has survived. However, that the Reagan period ended does not mean that U.S. imperialism has been defeated. On the contrary, the policies of the Bush administration require sophisticated adjustments by the Nicaraguan government and the liberation movements in the region.

As for the contradictions in the region, the Farabundo Marti National Liberation Front (FMLN) in El Salvador scored more and more military victories as the Christian Democratic government of Jose Napolean Duarte fell into further disarray amid splits in his party and charges of corruption. But significant support from the upper and middle classes, with some support from peasants, tilted toward the death-squad party – the Nationalist Republican Alliance (ARENA). In March 1989, ARENA won an election victory, and its presidential candidate, Alfredo Christiani, assumed office in June. The Bush administration made it clear that U.S. policy was to support the ARENA government, despite its violent record in El Salvador. With the expanding FMLN military capabilities and ARENA promises to slaughter the thousands of potential supporters of the guerrillas, it is not unlikely that at some point in the future the Bush administration might consider intervening more directly in the country to "save" it from the liberation movement.

In neighboring Honduras, popular opposition to the presence of the contras in base camps along the country's border with Nicaragua has been spreading ferment for change. People resent the U.S. role in the thorough militarization of Honduras, the illegal kidnapping by the United States of an alleged Honduran drug dealer from his home there, and the dispatch of several thousand U.S. troops to the country in March 1988, in response to a claimed incursion of Nicaraguan troops into Honduran territory. Death threats against leaders of opposition groups increased dramatically and there were several assassinations. Honduras seemed ripe for a broadening mass movement for change.

In Guatemala, the Christian Democratic government of Vinicio Cerezo has long refused to carry out any reforms in land holdings, taxes and social welfare. Despite the fact that Cerezo's constituency included the workers and peasants, who wanted and needed dramatic social change, his position was totally dependent on the support of the military. Even though the government acceded to the wishes of the military, there were attempted military coups in Guatemala in 1989. Presumably, the government had not been pursuing the slaughter of the peasant guerrilla opposition with sufficient vigor for the tastes of some military officers.

Like the rest of the region, Costa Rica experienced continued economic crisis; consequently, its government remained vulnerable to

U.S. pressures. President Arias expressed concern about the impact on the peace process of continuing U.S. support for the contras but he periodically also criticized the Nicaraguan government for flaws in its moves toward democratization. In 1989, John Hull – the U.S. citizen with large landholdings on the Costa Rican side of the border with Nicaragua, also an alleged gun runner, drug dealer and host to the contras in the south – was arrested for violating Costa Rican law. This arrest generated outcries not only from Hull's friends in the Republican Party but from some anti-contra Democrats as well.

President Arias sent an outraged letter to the U.S. Congress, expressing his anger at the attempt to influence Costa Rican law and to violate her national sovereignty. His reaction illustrates the ongoing contradictory behavior of Central American elites allied with the United States. The political leaders and ruling classes in Costa Rica, El Salvador, Guatemala and Honduras want to stamp out revolution in their countries and to weaken the revolutionary regime in Nicaragua as much as possible, but even they were angered by the crass way in which the United States interfered in their countries' military, political and economic affairs. Some of their anger reflected the broad-based spirit of nationalism and opposition to U.S. imperialism that pervade the region.

Out of this set of contradictions had come the Central American peace process, updated by the meeting of Central American presidents in February and August, 1989. At the February meeting the representatives of the five countries agreed to work toward dismantling the contras and reincorporating them into Nicaraguan society within two months. President Bush later pressured the Honduran government to violate the provisions of this agreement; its very existence was a source of embarrassment to an administration every bit as committed as its predecessor to a contra victory of some sort in Nicaragua. However, in August the Presidents met again and decided to dismantle the contra camps by December 1989.

In the United States itself, resistance to the Reagan-Bush Central America policy continued in 1988 and 1989. Occasionally, the Democratic party candidate for president, Michael Dukakis spoke in opposition to support for the contras, and U.S. citizens continued to indicate to pollsters their opposition to contra aid. However, there was less opposition to the policy of spending billions of dollars to prop up the Salvadoran government. The media in 1988 and 1989 continued to frame events in Central America as part of the East-West conflict, and as a struggle between democracy – as manifested in the four Central American governments – and the "dictatorship" they attributed to Nicaragua and the FMLN guerrillas.

The contradictions in the internal politics of the United States were reflected in the agreement of the Bush administration and congressional Democrats, in the spring of 1989, to provide continued "humanitarian aid" to the contras until elections in Nicaragua in February 1990. This new aid package violated the February agreements by the Central Americans to dismantle the contras, but the nominally anti-contra Democrats claimed the "humanitarian aid" constituted a commitment to urge the contras to leave Honduras and return home. For the Bush administration, it was hoped that the agreement would keep the contra threat alive.

Events in the region, of course, shaped the internal political and economic forces in Nicaragua. The war deescalated and the Nicaraguan government was able slowly and partially to transfer resources to other concerns, particularly after negotiations with the contras in the spring of 1988 led to a ceasefire, which the Nicaraguan government has honored. Contra kidnappings, sabotage and assassinations continued in 1988 and 1989; the contras still remaining in Nicaragua violated cease-fire promises. Still, the Nicaraguan government, out of economic and diplomatic necessity, pushed ahead with its reconstruction and peace-making efforts as if the war were totally over.

Essentially, the Nicaraguans had won the war, but their economy was devastated. Consequently, in 1988 and 1989, radical programs of economic austerity were put in place to reduce inflation and stimulate productivity in agriculture and manufacturing. These increased the peoples' suffering; in some areas, the government was not even able to maintain the status quo it sought in the survival economy.

Despite the broadly felt economic effects of the war, noted by us in 1987 and more apparent in the years to follow, no popular opposition to the FSLN-led government seems to have emerged. The opposition parties, growing to fifteen or twenty as factionalism increased, were unable to marshall substantial backing from the population. Support for the FSLN did seem to be declining because of the level of suffering in the cities and the countryside, but that did not produce the growth of any viable alternative political force. Observers of the Nicaraguan scene, even among the opposition, were predicting that the FSLN candidates would be victorious in the February 1990 elections.

The Central American Peace Process Continues: Esquipulas II, Sapoá, Esquipulas IV, and Tela

The Central American Peace Treaty accepted by the five regional presidents in August 1987 at Esquipulas established a set of commitments to national reconciliation, democratization and amnesty programs; to ending states of emergency within countries and outside interference in the affairs of the region; and to negotiations between guerrillas and governments to end ongoing civil wars. A series of measures were to be taken by the signatories during the first ninety days after the signing of the treaty and its success was to be evaluated in six months.

The Nicaraguan government has acted in ways supportive of the letter and spirit of Esquipulas, including initiation of national dialogue, ending the suspension of the opposition newspaper, *La Prensa,* and continuing the amnesty program to reincorporate contra fighters into Nicaraguan society. Despite the efforts of the press to minimize the significance of Nicaraguan moves from August 1987 to January 1988 to comply with the treaty, it was clear – even in *their* accounts – that Nicaragua was more fully in compliance than any other signatory. Honduras, for example, continued to deny that the contras were positioned in its country at all.

The Reagan-Bush administrations have repeatedly condemned the Nicaraguan government for non-compliance with the treaty and pressed on for continued contra aid, in the face of opposition from those who viewed support for the contras as a violation of the treaty provisions. From this latter point of view, the United States was and is the biggest violator of the treaty, as it continues to support the contra army against the government of Nicaragua and is the most significant outside source of military support for El Salvador, Honduras and Guatemala.

One provision of the peace treaty that is a further source of embarrassment to the United States and El Salvador, Guatemala and Honduras involved the establishment of an international verification commission whose task was to review the progress of the treaty from August 1987 to January 1988. Along with the foreign ministers of the five Central American countries, the commission included representatives of the eight-nation Contadora and Contadora support group, as well as from the United Nations and the Organization of American States. Four of the Central American countries would have preferred that representatives of other Latin American nations deemed "pro-Sandinista" not be included.

The commission issued its 150-page report in January 1988, when the presidents of the Central American countries met, assessing the successes and failures of the treaty's application. The *New York Times* dismissed the report without summarizing it by saying it was "pro-Sandinista." The *Los Angeles Times,* however, ran a story on January 14, 1988, based upon a leaked copy of the report's conclusions. The report emphasized that a "definitive halt" of United States aid to the contras was "an indispensable requirement for the success" of the peace process. It said that the continued deadlock in the peace process was largely the result of continued U.S. support of the contras and the non-compliance of the four U.S. allies with key treaty terms. According to the commission the Nicaraguan government had not fully complied with the terms of the treaty, but clearly they were not the stumbling block to success that was being claimed by the Reagan administration.

The report concluded that peace in Central America was being subverted by a "geopolitical struggle" of foreign interests. It said that Nicaragua had taken concrete steps toward democratization over the last five months; of the five countries, only Nicaragua's National Reconciliation Commission included representatives of government opponents. On a more critical side, from the newspaper's point of view, the report claimed that Nicaragua had refused to grant full amnesty to all contras until aid to them ended.

The *Los Angeles Times* article suggested that the commission report was to a considerable extent a consensus document, its tone affected by the presence of the Central American foreign ministers. Even so, the final report recommended an end to aid to the contras. However, at the January meeting of the Central American presidents, the verification commission was dissolved, with no reference made to its document. The newspaper made note of private comments by Central American officials that the Contadora countries were biased in favor of Nicaragua. In total, the commission report and its disposition reflected the continuing efforts by the United States and its allies in the region to crush the Nicaraguan revolution by diplomacy and information manipulation. The reality of Nicaragua, in this case its compliance with the peace process, made the job difficult.

At the end of the January 1988 Central American presidents' meeting, Daniel Ortega announced that the Nicaraguan government was prepared to begin direct negotiations with representatives of the contras and that the state of emergency in place for most of the period of the contra war would be ended. Also, a ban on several radio stations was lifted and the special tribunals used to try cases of those violating national security were abolished.

In March 1988, after several meetings between the contras and government representatives, President Ortega invited the contra leadership to meet in Nicaragua to move the negotiating process along. He appointed his brother, Defense Minister Humberto Ortega, to head the delegation to the meeting in Sapoá, a small town near the Costa Rican border. In February and March the U.S. Congress debated and rejected new military aid to the contras and a Democrat-sponsored "humanitarian" aid package. It was already clear to the contra leadership that military aid was not likely to be approved in the future and that the so-called humanitarian aid might be ended as well.

Perhaps most critically for the 1988 negotiations with the contras, the Nicaraguan military launched a large offensive called "Operation Danto" in early March. The ten-day operation on the northern border of Nicaragua combined land and air assaults and caught the contras by surprise; it forced most of the contra military forces from Nicaragua. After claiming that Nicaraguan forces had invaded Honduras, the Reagan administration sent 3,200 soldiers to that country's border with Nicaragua. Reagan probably feared that the Nicaraguans would finally destroy the base camps along the border.

In view of the defeats the contras were suffering in Congress and on the battlefield, they agreed to send a delegation to the proposed meeting at Sapoá on March 21, 1988. After two days, the contra and government negotiators signed the Sapoá agreement, with Cardinal Obando Y Bravo of Nicaragua and Joao Baena Soares, the secretary general of the OAS, observing.

The Sapoá agreement had several provisions. A sixty-day halt in offensive military operations was accepted. Contra forces would be moved to designated zones. Once in these zones, the contras would hand over their arms; they would then receive amnesty and would be invited to engage in national dialogue on the future of the country. A general amnesty would be decreed freeing those awaiting trial and those already sentenced for crimes against national security. Finally, the details of the accords were entrusted to a technical commission, and a final ceasefire agreement was to be completed within sixty days.

The Sapoá agreement projected the end of the tragic contra war, the reincorporation of contra fighters into Nicaraguan society, an end to the various emergency provisions in Nicaragua resulting from the war, and – specifically stated in the accords – a contra agreement to end receipt of military assistance from any source. Instead, the contras could receive only humanitarian aid "channeled through neutral organizations." This last point meant that future aid should be administered by an organization outside the direct control of the U.S. government.

Consequently, it was not surprising that the Reagan administration expressed skepticism about the accord and began pressuring sectors of the contra leadership to resist its provisions. Reagan was able to secure Congressional passage of an "humanitarian" aid measure for the contras in April as well as some funds for war orphans and for verification of the carrying out of the Sapoá agreement. He also encouraged contra negotiators to make new demands on the Nicaraguan government and to resist final agreements on contra relocation and incorporation into Nicaraguan society. The contras refused to accept the International Red Cross as a neutral organization for the distribution of humanitarian aid and the U.S. government began using the State Department's Agency for International Development (AID) as the conduit for their newly approved aid despite Nicaraguan government protests that such actions violated the terms of the treaty. Also, contra leaders refused to provide information on the number and whereabouts of the hundreds of Nicaraguans kidnapped and held prisoner by the contras.

In April and May, factional fighting among contra leaders increased. U.S. officials, like Assistant Secretary of State Elliot Abrams, and representatives of the CIA urged the most hardline elements to resist the accords. Finally victorious in the internecine struggle was Colonel Enrique Bermudez, who had opposed the Sapoá agreement from the outset. Bermudez was able to scuttle the accords with his own grandiose demands, plus support and pressure from the United States. By June the contras had withdrawn from all negotiations, to the great disappointment of the Nicaraguan people. Afterwards, contra leaders met with President Reagan in Washington, where he declared the negotiations a sham designed to weaken contra forces.

Having once again derailed the peace process, the U.S. government moved in new ways to destroy the Nicaraguan government. Secretary of State Shultz visited the four Central American countries allied with the United States to pressure them to work more vigorously against Nicaragua. Threats were matched with promises of more economic and military assistance. Inside Nicaragua, the Bishop's Conference demanded an "urgent change" in the country, and opposition parties and the business sector called for a "Government of National Salvation." The U.S. assault on the revolution was to continue, with or without the contras.

The Nicaraguan government repeatedly announced extensions of the ceasefire agreed to at Sapoa, but contra acts of terror resumed in July. They mined roads, attacked civilian transport, and ambushed army troops in various parts of the country. In July, nine people were killed, nine wounded, and 187 kidnapped by the contras. While the scale of violence against the people had declined, and while the government was reordering priorities from defense to the economy, death and destruction continued.

With the active involvement of U.S. embassy personnel, a group of anti-government activists attacked local police during a July demonstration in Nandaime, forty miles south of Managua. The rock-throwing government critics, with their U.S. advisers, were eager to provoke a police reaction. Several demonstration leaders were arrested and the

U.S. ambassador was expelled from Nicaragua because of the embassy's role in the disorder and its other attempts to organize opposition to the government. In reprisal, President Reagan ordered Carlos Tunnermann, Nicaragua's ambassador to the United States and the OAS, to leave Washington.

In August 1988, Secretary of State Shultz returned to Central America, hoping to secure a jointly signed communique blaming Nicaragua for the failures of the peace process. This effort failed. The administration was able to secure $27 million in "humanitarian" aid for the contras in September and $25.3 million in transport and insurance for the shipment of arms previously acquired, $5 million in medicines for the Catholic hierarchy and $2 million for opposition parties inside Nicaragua. The package also included a provision to free $16.3 million in military aid passed in 1987 if the Nicaraguan government were to launch an offensive against contra forces in the country. The militarily spent and politically isolated contras thus received an aid package that totaled about $75.6 million. It was not surprising, therefore, that they refused to accept the Nicaraguan government's offer to resume negotiations.

Further, Speaker of the House James Wright confirmed what Nicaraguan officials had been claiming for years, that the CIA was involved in convert operations such as creating and supporting anti-government demonstrations and rock-throwing melees in Nicaragua to destabilize the government. In response to the increased U.S. interference in the internal affairs of the country, the National Assembly passed a law in October 1988 prohibiting individuals and groups from accepting the monies from the United States that came from the various contra aid packages.

George Bush was elected President in November 1988 and proclaimed his hostility to the Nicaraguan government and his support for the contras. Over the next several months administration spokespersons indicated that they would not be asking for military aid for the contras, largely because the Democratic majorities in the House and Senate would vote against it. However, the administration would seek to construct a bipartisan consensus to achieve as damaging a program against Nicaragua as Congress and the citizens would allow.

Also in November 1988, the Central American presidents agreed to hold a summit meeting in January 1989 to discuss the peace process. Proposals had been discussed in the OAS and among the foreign ministers of the region to have representatives from outside countries monitor the borders between Honduras, El Salvador and Nicaragua. Other proposals surfaced to establish verification teams that would check to see if countries were being used as staging areas for attacks on others in the region. Costa Rica and Nicaragua signed an agreement for jointly patrolling their common border.

When President Arias of Costa Rica called for postponing the January summit meeting of the heads of state, to give President Bush time to take office and assess U.S. policy in the region, pessimism surfaced about whether the meeting would occur at all. However, in early February, the Central American presidents did meet in San Salvador and, to the surprise of the Bush administration, signed another agreement – known as Esquipulas IV because it continued the peace process begun in that city.

The most critical feature of the Esquipula IV agreement was its call for dismantling the contra insurgents and reincorporating them into Nicaraguan society. Specifically, the agreement called for the following:

1. Continued commitment to all the provisions of prior peace treaties
2. Nicaragua would advance the date for its next elections to no later than February 25, 1990;
3. Nicaragua would carry out electoral and media reforms to insure a fair election, the process to be monitored by representatives from the UN and OAS;
4. Nicaragua would release prisoners designated by the human rights commission of the OAS;
5. Within 90 days a plan would be drawn up to demobilize, repatriate or relocate contras currently housed in Honduras;
6. An end to all outside support for insurrectionary movements in Central America, except for humanitarian aid that did not interfere with the peace process;
7. An appeal to outside countries to help in the social and econmic recovery of the region;
8. The Central American nations would act in concert to end drug trafficking in the region;
9. The presidents would meet again at some time in the future.

Once again, the U.S. government was caught off guard and real national interests of the Central Americans surfaced. The Hondurans were eager to extricate the contra force from their territory because of its destabilizing effects on their political process and economy; the Costa Ricans wished to reduce direct U.S. intervention, which always threatened to expand into a regionwide war; and the Nicaraguans demanded an end to the military force that still engaged in violence, terror and destruction against its population. It seemed that at last the contras would be demobilized, the war would be over, and the Nicaraguan people could commit all of their resources to economic reconstruction, having suffered billions of dollars' worth of destruction and thousands of deaths in eight years of war.

Unfortunately, U.S. policymakers still wanted to maintain a contra army as a threat to the Nicaraguans, forcing their continued diversion of resources from vital economic needs. President Bush pressured the Honduran government to renege on its Esquipulas IV commitment to dismantle the contras, and he secured from Congress a new "humanitarian" aid package for the contras, clearly in violation of the letter and spirit of the treaty. Bush was able to get from the foreign ministers of four of the signatory countries agreement that the continued presence of the contras in Honduras did not constitute a violation of the treaty terms. They accepted the U.S. interpretation that the $67 million contra aid package would support their demobilization until such time as they chose to return to Nicaragua, such return to be when conditions in Nicaragua improved.

Democrats who had opposed contra aid in the past thought this aid package would insure demobilization of the contras and hailed the bipartisan agreement as a victory for peace in the region. However, the Bush administration made it clear that it expected the contra forces to stay in place until after the February 1990 elections in Nicaragua. It wanted the contras to serve as a threat to the Nicaraguan government to carry out the democratic elections promised in Esquipulas IV.

But when the Nicaraguan national assembly passed election reform laws and talked of establishing an electoral council to oversee the 1990 elections, the Bush administration began to complain that the elections would not be democratic. Of course, the only elections the United States would define as democratic would be those in which the FSLN lost; any other choice made by the Nicaraguan people would be unacceptable. Bush was eager to keep the contras in place – if not to fight again, then at least to continue to require diversion of Nicaraguan resources from economic needs to defense. The new administration had not changed the historic goals of U.S. imperialism.

Bush administration goals continued to be thwarted, however, on August 8, 1989 as a result of another meeting of the Central American presidents at Tela, Honduras. At this most recent meeting, the presidents called foa complete demobilization of the contras by December 5, 1989; contras could either be repatriated to Nicaragua or relocated to other nations in the hemisphere. A commission to oversee and support the demobilization selected by the UN and

OAS was to be established. A central stimulus for this accord was a united call by both the Nicaraguan government and opposition political parties for the dismantling of the contras just days before the Tela meeting. All political forces in the region, except the United States and the contras, had finally come to the view that the violence and destruction in Nicaragua must cease.

U.S. foreign policy for the ten years of the Nicaraguan revolution has reflected a tenacious struggle, using whatever means possible, to destroy the people's government. Even when Congress forbade U.S. aid to the contras in their effort to overthrow the Nicaraguan government under the so-called Boland Amendment (in force from 1984 to 1986), the Reagan administration chose to ignore the law and raised money for the contras.

The Iran/contra scandal which surfaced in the fall of 1986 illustrated the fanaticism and secrecy embedded in the dynamics of imperialism. Reagan administrators sold arms to Iran through intermediaries and used the profits made from those sales to transfer funds for weapons to the contras. Also, the administration solicited other countries, such as Israel and Saudi Arabia, to support the contra cause. Further, the White House encouraged private organizations like the World Anti-Communist League to raise funds for their beloved "freedom fighters." These illegal activities had been exposed and protested by a variety of progressive groups and publications, but not until the Iran/contra scandal broke did the U.S. media begin to cover the story.

Congress investigated the illegalities and identified a small number of persons like Colonel Oliver North and John Poindexter as perpetrators of the crimes. The Democratic majorities in Congress were not eager to expose the illegalities and the links between the President, Vice President and other key decisionmakers, nor did they wish to present information that would encourage U.S. citizens to put the pieces of the puzzle together in such a way that the structure of U.S. imperialism would be uncovered. Consequently, the investigation only scratched the surface of the scandal; the covert operations, private fundraising, third-country contributions and "humanitarian" aid to the contras continued. Overt support for the military dictators in El Salvador, Guatemala and Honduras was not challenged.

Reflecting upon these events should make sensitive observers skeptical about signs of change in U.S. foreign policy. Progressives rightly celebrated the exit of Ronald Reagan from the White House. George Bush had often been characterized as a chameleon during his political career, but media pundits suggested that the new administration would carry out a more "pragmatic, less doctrinaire" foreign policy.

They implied that the new administration would not pursue the Reagan Doctrine, would not work to overthrow progressive governments around the world. However, any hope of some change in U.S. policy was dashed and frustrated by several early Bush moves. His administration violated the agreements made with the Soviet Union and Pakistan concerning Afghanistan. While the Soviet Union was withdrawing all its troops from Afghanistan, the United States increased aid to the Afghan rebels and urged them to secure a military victory over the government in Kabul. The CIA and the U.S. media assumed that the Afghan government would collapse as soon as the Soviet troops were removed. To their dismay this did not happen. Only after major offensives by the rebels failed did the administration indicate its willingness to have them negotiate a ceasefire, still demanding that any new Afghan government would have to exclude members of the current government, which constituted a demand for the Afghan government to surrender.

The Bush administration continued to support the forces of Jonas Savimbi, or UNITA, which were fighting against the government of Angola. Here was another contra-style war, less visible to people in the United States but equally as murderous to the local population as the war in Central America. Support for UNITA also violated the recently completed negotiations between Angola, Cuba and South Africa for Namibian independence.

The Bush administration cóntinued to harass the government of Panama and organized a crusade against the elections held there in the spring of 1989. Much funding and exhortation of Panamanians occurred for weeks before the election to encourage them to defeat candidates supported by General Manuel Noriega. The United States sent delegates to "observe" the election and after it was over – but before results were tabulated – declared the opposition to Noriega victorious. Opposition protests were organized as the government in power moved to declare the election void. The United States then tried to mobilize other nations to condemn the Panamanian government for its disdain for democratic elections.

Throughout the period since the elections were held and voided, the Bush administration clearly implied that military intervention to protect "democracy" in Panama was being considered. The media always presented the Panamanian issue from the point of view of the administration, never questioning the right of the United States to interfere in the internal affairs of neighboring countries. The whole mad crusade for democracy in Panama (but not in South Africa or South Korea) was a prelude to the attacks on the Nicaraguan elections that will take place in February 1990. In fact, Bush and other politicians cited Nicaragua's new election laws as proof that it was following in the same path as Panama.

The Nicaraguan government has urged the United States to engage in direct dialogue to settle outstanding issues. This appeal was made again as recently as June 1989. The response of the Bush administration was that it would not talk to Nicaragua until it held democratic elections. The United States was not willing to consider normal diplomatic exchange as an option.

In fact, the Bush administration has worked to keep the contras alive as a military threat, using the bipartisan "humanitarian" aid project to do just that.

The Bush administration has continued the practice of funneling funds to anti-government factions in Nicaragua through the National Endowment for Democracy and other overt arms of U.S. imperialism. The newspaper *La Prensa,* Cardinal Obando Y Bravo, the Nicaraguan association of private enterprise (COSEP), a variety of small anti-government political parties, and the tiny AFL–CIO-supported trade union federation (CUS)* have all been recipients of funds to destabilize the current government. Finally, Congress has authorized $5 million to support opposition parties as they prepare for the 1990 Nicaraguan elections.

This interference in the internal life of an independent country is taken for granted by the administration, the media and too many citizens of the United States. None of these would be so sanguine if the Soviet Union, Cuba or Nicaragua funded political activities in the United States. In fact, one of the charges made against domestic opponents of U.S. policies, historically, has been that they were funded from abroad, and consequently were un-American.

In fact, under the rubric of fighting communism, "low-intensity conflict," and whatever else Bush's policies are now called, U.S. policy around the world since World War II has been motivated by a commitment to extend monopoly capitalist control and defend it, to oppose socialism, and oppose national self-determination if it weakened U.S. imperialism. Policymakers have used direct military intervention, threats of conventional and nuclear war, economic blockades, discriminatory patterns of aid and trade, and diplomatic pressure to weaken and if possible destroy socialist and some new nationalist governments.

In response, the latter have been forced to engage in costly defense programs, institute security measures that impair democracy, and make national survival – not economic growth and human need fulfillment – their number one priority. The Bush administration, therefore, is continuing the policy of opposing change, and impeding the thrust toward peace and progress around the world. The years ahead

*See also p. 41.

will determine the success or failure of the Nicaraguan people to overcome the enormous obstacles placed by U.S. imperialism. In the United States, there is a need for people who are now struggling against Bush policies on a wide front – labor's and women's rights, for civil liberties, against racism and for peace – to connect these demands more firmly to a curbing of adventurous U.S. foreign policy in Latin America.

Economic Crisis in Nicaragua

Of course, the negative impacts of the war on the Nicaraguan economy have been enormous. Increasingly, resources for health, education, food production and consumption, construction, and industrial production have had to be diverted, reversing some of the people's gains under the revolution.

According to standard indicators of economic performance reported in *Envio*,* Nicaragua's negative trade balance grew through out the 1980s, but particularly from 1985 to 1988. Foreign debt has increased markedly over the last three years. Per capita gross domestic product, which increased during three of the first five years of the revolution, declined from 1985 through 1988 by 7.3, 3.9, 1.7, and 12.1 percent respectively. Perhaps the most glaring economic problem faced by the Nicaraguans is rampant inflation – for 1988 it was estimated at 22,000 percent.

The U.S. press has gleefully reported the economic problems of the Nicaraguan government, and ideologues have charged that these resulted from mismanagement. Supine before the monopolies – and part of the monopoly structure – they attribute the problems of the Nicaraguan economy to those of its policies providing workers and peasants with basic services for the first time, rather than mention the $12 billion worth of U.S.-directed destruction during the contra war, or the U.S. economic blockade.

While the war and the blockade are clearly the cause of the vast majority of problems, such as declining productivity, shortages and inflation, the FSLN-led government came to the view that further policy responses to the crisis were needed. In February 1988, the government announced the first measures to reduce inflation, stimulate agricultural productivity among small- and medium-sized producers, reduce black market activities, and to encourage collaboration with the country's private sector. These first reforms included devaluation with the creation of a new currency, unification of several exchange rates, and some upward adjustment of wages.

Envio is the monthly magazine of the Instituto Historico Centroamericano.

Then the government began a difficult reexamination of the state sector and its policy of giving credits to borrowers, with an eye toward reducing the government's budget deficit. In June, price controls were eliminated on most commodities; the government, however, continued to guarantee certain base levels for rice and beans, the staples for workers.

Further adjustments continued during the summer of 1988, including reductions in taxes on imports, rescheduling of ranchers' debts, and a further devaluation of the currency. Prices of gasoline and diesel fuel were raised and subsidies on electricity and water were withdrawn. Wage increases were approved.

In October, the *cordoba* was devalued for a third time in the year. Unfortunately, in that month, economic reform was interrupted by the incredible devastation of Hurricane Joan, which leveled towns along the Atlantic coast of Nicaragua and had effects throughout the country.

The hurricane caused losses worth $1.6 billion as it brought down thousands of trees in eastern forest lands. Thirty thousand homes were destroyed and 180,000 Nicaraguans were made homeless. Even committed revolutionaries began to ask how much more destruction and how many more setbacks the people would have to endure before their lives could again begin to improve.

The Nicaraguan government instituted a number of emergency measures to facilitate recovery on the Atlantic coast and elsewhere where damage was severe. It provided flexible credit programs, donated seed for planting, postponed loan repayments, reduced interest rates for those in the damage area, reduced taxes for those business people who donated money for hurricane relief, and provided special funds for planting programs. Assistance was provided by several countries, with Cuba leading the way. While solidarity workers in the United States raised significant amounts of material aid, the U.S. government made *no* contribution of assistance and proclaimed that Nicaragua had exaggerated the damage.

Resuming the economic austerity program, the Nicaraguan government devalued the currency again in November 1988 while adjusting public employee wage levels slightly upward. On January 30, 1989, President Daniel Ortega announced the next dramatic phase of the economic program, indicating the need to strengthen Nicaragua's mixed economy and to create more cooperation between workers, business people and the state.

This phase would include transforming some state companies into privately or jointly owned enterprises, reducing the national budget deficit by 11.3 percent, cutting the national budget by 20 percent, cutting back on government investments, reducing loan programs to those recipients who can pay them back, cutting the number of government employees, selling or renting government-owned houses, adjusting wages to production levels, further progress toward one exchange rate and an end to the black market.

There would be reduced state intrusion in the economy, significant reductions in state expenditures – such as a 29 percent cut in the Ministry of Defense budget and a 40 percent cut in the Ministry of Interior budget – removal of thousands of employees from the state payroll, and a further move toward market-driven prices for most basic commodities. Ortega recognized that this program would increase the sacrifices made by the Nicaraguan people, that credit would be more scarce, unemployment would increase, and the expanded social services of the 1980s would be reduced. He argued, as did many non-FSLN economists, that this austerity program and stimulation of the mixed economy were necessary to overcome the problems of hyperinflation and economic stagnation that Nicaragua had been experiencing since 1985.

Envio analyzed the economic austerity programs of 1988 and 1989 in its May 1989 issue. From their perspective as sympathetic critics of the revolution, they characterized the economic austerity as necessary to overcome the country's problems – enlarged services to the population, expenditures necessitated by the contra war, the limited amount of outside assistance and loans available to the government and bias favoring urban businesses and workers in policies of the 1980s.

Envio claimed that progressive critics of the austerity program were incorrect to assume that the Nicaraguan government had adopted International Monetary Fund-type programs that would diminish, rather than enhance, the prospects for building a people's economy. Rather, they held, the tighter controls on credit would lead to a greater flow of loans to small and medium farm producers rather than the traditional capitalist bourgeoisie, and market-driven prices would increase the motivation of these small agricultural producers to expand their production. To *Envio,* the small landholders and the participants in cooperatives who are represented in UNAG, the ranchers and farmers organization, may serve – given Nicaragua's circumstances – as the leading force for development in the future.

Indeed, the programs put in place by the Sandinista government have generated much debate within Nicaragua as well as among supporters outside. As some have pointed out, these austerity programs have been promulgated by a government whose goal is the advancement of the population as a whole. One measure of the broad acceptance of this proposition is comparison of Nicaraguan reactions to the announced programs with those of the people in countries like Venezuela, where austerity measures were met with urban riots and subsequent police repression. If the measures are successful in the long run, as is believed by many Nicaraguans, the people will reap the benefits, not an economic ruling class or a political elite.

Nicaraguans React to War, Revolution and Economic Crisis

One of our concerns as we traveled in Nicaragua in 1987 was to note the level of support for the revolution. Our assessments of the high level of that support and the even higher levels of opposition to the U.S.-created contras came from a variety of partial but interesting sources. During our two-week visit, we spoke with government officials, a U.S. citizen working in the human rights commission, friends of our guide, the landlady where our guide lived, and others. We also looked for signs of protest – marches, public fights, graffiti – that might indicate disenchantment with the government, but we heard criticisms of the government only during our first full day in the country, at the party for us attended by wealthy Nicaraguans.

Obviously, criticisms of the government did exist, as did support, both ideological and material, for the contras. There are opposition parties in Nicaragua, and the members of the association of private enterprise (COSEP) represent, along with the newspaper *La Prensa,* loud voices of criticism of the government. Since our visit, we heard and read about growing disenchantment with the government among the population, fueled by the deepening economic difficulties and the continuation of the contra attacks. The general goal of U.S. policy is to so bleed the country, literally and figuratively, that growing numbers of Nicaraguans, out of sheer exhaustion and despair, would turn against their revolution.

The question of what Nicaraguans think about their revolution and the war was studied systematically for the first time in June 1988. The University of Central America, a Jesuit school, in conjunction with the Interamerican Research Center, which has offices in Los Angeles and Mexico City and does polls in Central America, carried out a survey on June 4 and 5, 1988 of Nicaraguans living in Managua. A representative sample of 1,129 Nicaraguans from 70 neighborhoods in Managua were interviewed in their homes on a variety of issues. The pollsters, advised by independent experts, developed sampling procedures to represent the variety of people in the Managua area as to age, class, gender, political orientation and level of information.

The interviews occurred during the last (unsuccessful) phase of the dialogue between the contras and the government to achieve a final cessation of hostilities. The week before the survey, contra representatives had withdrawn from negotiations; Colonel Bermudez, the contra leader most opposed to negotiations, was reasserting his control. However, as yet neither side had indicated that the negotiations had failed. In the field, contras were still attacking civilians, although the amount of fighting had declined.

As to the economy, credit for agricultural producers had become more available in May, the rainy season had begun, planting was proceeding; monthly inflation rates had declined from 100 percent in February to 20 percent in May. Finally, the survey occurred before the announcements later in June of the second phase of the austerity program. Despite the temporary respite, the survey was taken at a time when Nicaraguans were experiencing severe economic problems.

When asked what they viewed as most responsible for the war, 47 percent of those surveyed blamed the United States or the contras, and only 16 percent blamed the FSLN. Eighty-five percent opposed contra aid and 72 percent said the government was interested in seeking peace. Fifty-two percent said the government was living up to the Esquipulas peace process (33 percent disagreed).

As for reactions to the United States, 62 percent of respondents rated U.S. policies as "bad" or "terrible," and the United States was ranked as the country "that least seeks peace in Central America." When asked what they most admired about the United States, 42 percent said nothing. When asked about what is most disliked about the United States, 47 percent said imperialism, war-making or aggression.

For comparison, respondents were asked to evaluate other countries relevant to Nicaragua. Fourteen percent said Cuban policy toward Nicaragua was excellent, 40 percent said good, 16 percent said fair. The policy of Mexico was judged excellent by 8 percent, good by 46 percent, and fair by 21 percent. Finally, Soviet foreign policy toward Nicaragua was judged excellent by 14 percent, good by 43 percent and fair by 14 percent.

Nicaraguans surveyed were more critical of the condition of the economy. Seventy-four percent said their economic situation was worse than a year before. The way the government handled the economy was rated excellent by 2 percent, good by 20 percent, fair by 36 percent, bad by 24 percent and terrible by 14 percent.

The government's political performance over the last nine years was rated excellent by 6 percent of the respondents, good by 21 percent, fair by 41 percent, bad by 15 percent, and terrible by 11 percent. When asked which party they identified with, 28 percent said the FSLN, 3 percent the Liberal party, 3 percent the Social Christian party and 3 percent the Conservative party. Fifty-nine percent of the respondents said that they identified with no political party.

Those surveyed were asked opinions on some controversial issues. Seventy percent said the Sandinista-led government is seeking peace (24 percent said no). Fifty-seven percent agreed with the current relationship between the FSLN, the state, and the armed forces (31 percent disagreed). Forty-eight percent of those surveyed said the neighborhood community organizations (the CDSs) should exist, while 47 percent disagreed. Forty-three percent favored continuation of the draft, 53 percent disagreed. Forty percent of the respondents said the FSLN government was democratic, 48 percent said it was not. Eighty-three percent of respondents felt there should be partial or total amnesty for contra supporters, and 39 percent believed that properties confiscated by the government should be returned (34 percent said no, 22 percent "just some").

The portrait from this poll of residents of Managua is a complex one. First, the data indicate that Nicaraguans overwhelmingly oppose United States foreign policy *and* the contras. Further, many Nicaraguans appreciate the support given to the Nicaraguan revolution by the Soviet Union, Cuba and Mexico. Perhaps surprisingly, the data suggest that many Nicaraguans have a deep disdain for the United States, probably nourished during the years of Somoza rule and exacerbated by the contra war.

Second, more Nicaraguans than supported U.S. policy and the contras were critical of their government's handling of the economy. A vast majority of Nicaraguans had experienced worsening economic situations in the recent past.

Third, while support for the FSLN exceeded that for any other party, a majority of respondents indicated that they had no party preference. At the point of the survey, there did not exist any opposition political force that was a threat to the FSLN. Despite the lack of identification with the FSLN, more Nicaraguans evaluated positively Daniel Ortega's performance as President (11 percent excellent, 31 percent good, 29 percent fair, 14 percent poor, 7 percent very bad).

Fourth, on specific issues, many Nicaraguans surveyed disapproved of the CDSs and/or the draft, supported amnesty for contras, and wanted confiscated lands returned. However, a sizable majority were satisfied with the links between party, state and military.

Despite the war, the economic crisis, and the first phase of the austerity program, this survey suggests that the Reagan-Bush strategy of bleeding the revolution to death has failed so far. Nicaraguans surveyed reflected a degree of skepticism about their leaders, the revolutionary party and significant policies, but gave no indication that they were prepared to opt for any other alternative to the current leadership.

Bob Teclaw and Jan Beckstrand have returned to Nicaragua twice after our June 1987 visit. They were in Nicaragua for two weeks during February 1988, and again for two weeks in March 1989. On these trips Bob and Jan were less tourists than workers in their areas of specialty in support of Nicaraguan government programs.

In his 1988 trip, Bob worked under the auspices of Tecnica in the animal health office affiliated with the Ministry of Agriculture. He helped prepare a system of reporting on animal diseases that could facilitate the ministry's learning about the problems and needs of the farmers and ranchers. During his stay he had occasion to visit a variety of farming communities south and west of Managua, including a large state-owned dairy. Bob's next visit, in March 1989, was under the auspices of a private organization, the Heffer Project International, and involved his working for CEPAD, a Protestant material aid group. Bob taught animal technicians about veterinary medicine, visiting farms west, south and east of Managua as part of his work.

During both trips Jan was under the auspices of Tecnica. She taught research design and statistical methods, and consulted for the National Autonomous University in Managua. In her second visit, she gave short courses on sampling techniques and statistics at the medical school and consulted on a survey of mortality rates of children under six years of age.

Tecnica was founded during the escalating U.S. war against Nicaragua by concerned scientists who wanted to offer their skills to the Nicaraguan people. People with valuable scientific, engineering, statistical, language, construction, electronic and other skills are placed in various Nicaraguan governmental agencies for a period of two weeks or more to work for the people. Initially, Bob and Jan had written to the organization and completed its questionnaire, designed to screen out persons without usable skills or the commitment to do disciplined work for a period of time. Tecnica sought reliable and committed people with useful skills, but did not require applicants to hold any particular political perspective.

For the first trip, Bob and Jan assembled with 30 delegates in Mexico City before proceeding to Nicaragua. Volunteers receive assignments one month before their trips and are encouraged also to bring material aid – medical supplies, books, school materials, etc. – with them. Most of those going to Nicaragua with Bob and Jan were engineers, health care workers and translators. Tecnica affords concerned North Americans useful opportunities to offer themselves for service to Nicaragua.

I was eager to get my friends' perceptions of the situation in Nicaragua, particularly as we had shared experiences and perspectives from our earlier trip. Recently, I asked them to discuss Nicaragua's economic and political condition to see if their reports sustained the data in the survey I had read.

Economically, Bob and Jan said, the condition of Nicaragua had worsened since 1987. People spoke of malnutrition during their most recent visit, and they had heard stories of Nicaraguans going hungry. Reports of such sufferings had appeared in the newspapers as well. In part, the malnutrition resulted from cutbacks on state subsidies of food and the devaluations of the currency. Prices for commodities in Managua were comparable to U.S. prices, but salaries were not at all equivalent. Bob said that Nicaraguans needed alternative sources of income, along with their regular jobs, to survive.

Other indicators of the depths of the economic crisis were the appearance for the first time of children begging in the streets and the increased incidents of crime, particularly against foreigners. In 1987, it was commonly believed that anyone could walk the streets of Managua anytime, anyplace. Bob and Jan reported that this was no longer true.

From what they heard and saw, people were more desperate. Incomes had declined, jobs were lost in the austerity program, and it was very difficult for the government to convince Nicaraguans to relocate in the countryside to engage in agriculture. People would not be motivated to produce more if they could not afford to purchase commodities because the money they earned was worth so little.

Jan reported on the state of health care in 1989. Infant mortality rates had increased over the last two years and tuberculosis was on the rise. Malnutrition was decreasing people's power to resist diseases that only a few years earlier had been dramatically reduced.

Further, medicines were scarce as were skilled medical personnel, including teachers for the medical school. Bob and Jan brought a hotplate with them on the most recent trip, to be used to pasteurize infant formula in a hospital. It was a rare and treasured commodity. As for lack of medications, basic illnesses could not be treated because of the scarcities; various pain medications were scarce, so that those suffering from diseases and/or the after effects of surgery would experience extreme pain. Finally, Jan said, some health professionals were leaving the country to escape the shortages and the lack of desired income.

I asked them to discuss their views on the political implications of the economic crisis, mindful of the somewhat ambiguous but largely supportive attitude toward the government reflected in the UCA survey. Bob and Jan reported that there was no support for the contras;

while an opposition existed, they had not encountered any representatives of it.

The opposition newspaper, *La Prensa,* was read around the country, most intensively in selected areas like Chontales province, where support for the government was historically weak. Habitual newspaper readers would have no choice but to buy *La Prensa,* since it was the only afternoon newspaper. Bob reported that *La Prensa* printed lies, and often erroneous stories would be followed the next day by factual refutations from the morning newspapers, *Barricada* and *Nueva Diario.* But *La Prensa* would never issue retractions, even when stories were clearly proven wrong. Generally, Bob felt that *La Prensa* was not taken seriously, even by the opposition to the FSLN. One U.S. journalist told him that *La Prensa* was more effective for the opposition when shut down than when printing regularly.

Other indicators of opposition – graffiti, protest marches, etc. – were insignificant. Isolated marches such as the one at Nandaime orchestrated by the U.S. embassy in July 1988 were probably more significant politically in the United States than in Nicaragua.

As to the response and activities of the FSLN and the government, my friends said that they seemed to be popular. There were no demonstrations and riots after the various austerity measures were announced in Nicaragua as there had been in Venezuela at about the same time. Bob and Jan noted no signs of political repression. Daniel Ortega appeared at rallies without visible bodyguards standing between him and the people, except in Chontales province. Various leaders of the FSLN appeared often in public to engage in dialogue with the people.

In general, Bob felt that the people seemed relatively happy. There were no visible signs of a breakdown of social order. People seemed to come to work on time. Managua still had electricity, and water was provided to residents five days a week as had been the case in 1987. Considering the variety of historical and conjunctural constraints, the government and schools seemed to be run relatively efficiently.

Given the inadequacies in the economy and the impacts of the long war on the fabric of social life, Bob felt that it was remarkable that the government seemed to work as well as it did and that the seeming level of support for it remained. Also, he was amazed at the will and determination of the FSLN to persevere in the face of war, economic crisis and natural disaster. Jan drew a parallel with Vietnam. The Nicaraguan people had won the war, as had the Vietnamese, but the devastation had left them suffering and with a historically monumental task of rebuilding their society.

International Solidarity

So the people of Nicaragua continue to struggle against the disasters, human-made and natural, that plagued them after my 1987 visit. Support for the Nicaraguan government from solidarity groups, non-governmental organizations and nations continued. We had seen indicators of international support throughout our visit in 1987; reports from the media and such publications as *Barricada Internacional* and *Envio* confirmed its existence in 1988 and 1989.

International support came from Scandinavian governments, and socialist countries, particularly the Soviet Union, and Cuba. Where governments made only modest financial contributions to economic development or hurricane relief, progressive citizens of those countries – such as Italy and West Germany – provided support and personnel for Nicaragua.

As for hurricane relief specifically, the Cuban government had begun provisioning even before the winds touched down on Nicaraguan soil and over the next several weeks sent 23 planeloads of aid to Bluefields. In November, the Cubans donated 1,000 houses – complete with electricity, water and sewage – and a school, health center, and church, and promised to send 300 brigadistas over the next two years to build these structures. In total, the Cubans expected to provide 1,000 tons of aid for hurricane victims.

The Soviet Union sent 40,000 tons of rice, worth $30 million, and a boatload of supplies from the Soviet Red Cross. The Swedish government donated $3 million and the FRG (West Germany) $2 million. Other countries providing hurricane relief aid included Argentina, Belgium, Czechoslovakia, and the GDR (East Germany), France, Great Britain, Italy, Mexico, Panama, Spain, Switzerland and Uruguay.

When hurricane Gilbert earlier touched down on Jamaica, the United States sent $125 million in food and other aid. But the U.S. government contributed *nothing* for hurricane relief to Nicaragua.

Aid to Nicaragua has come through non-governmental organizations also. During the ten years of the revolution, hundreds of representatives of European and North American NGOs have worked in Nicaragua on a variety of community and agricultural development projects, small-scale industry, health and education. Some 70 NGOs have permanent offices in Nicaragua and they cooperate with Nicaraguan organizations. In recent years the NGOs and their Nicaraguan counterparts have tried to increase coordination of their efforts so that those providing funds and equipment can more effectively be matched with those providing skilled personnel.

U.S. citizens have been active in a variety of such organizations to provide material aid in general, and hurricane assistance in 1988 and 1989. Such organizations as Quest for Peace and the Nicaragua Network raise funds and collect material aid and transport it to Nicaragua. Organizations such as Tecnica, Heffer International and Operation California mobilize skilled personnel to spend time in Nicaragua working on a variety of projects.

Individual states, cities and towns identify specific projects and raise funds or in-kind aid, or mobilize people to work in Nicaragua with Nicaraguans on projects there. For example, the Fort Wayne, Indiana, community had raised funds for the addition to the health clinic at San Rafael del Sur in 1987; it completed the fund raising and sent a delegation of construction workers to build a much needed addition in January 1988. Solidarity groups in the Midwest participated in the collection of material aid on at least two occasions, sending goods in containers by boat to Nicaragua.

A few such efforts gained general visibility because of efforts of the Reagan administration to halt them. In the spring of 1988, a group of Vietnam veterans organized a convoy of trucks and buses filled with material aid to be driven to Nicaragua. The Nicaraguans were to receive the aid and keep the usable but battered vehicles. At the Mexican border, police on orders from the U.S. Treasury Department refused to allow the convoy to proceed until members provided a $100,000 bond guaranteeing that the trucks and buses would be returned. The government argued that the vehicles were not humanitarian aid and consequently leaving them in Nicaragua would violate the 1985 embargo.

After days of conflict with local authorities, part of the convoy drove to Washington, D.C., to protest in front of the Capitol. After legal action, the convoy was finally allowed to proceed. Of some 60 vehicles, 30 traveled through Mexico, Guatemala and Honduras and reached their Nicaraguan destination in the summer.

What all these efforts at solidarity suggest is that large numbers of progressive people – in formal organizations and as individuals – are committed to the survival of the Nicaragua revolution. What U.S. imperialism seeks to take away, the Nicaraguan people and their allies refuse to give up – the right to political and economic self-determination. Tiny Nicaragua has become a setting for the struggle between those who represent the past and those who represent and work for the future.

Ten Years of Revolution

Three hundred thousand Nicaraguans and solidarity workers from around the world celebrated the 10-year survival of the Nicaraguan revolution in Managua on July 19, 1989; millions more recognized the date in their own countries. Those of us who support the just struggles of peoples liberating themselves from imperialism know that each liberation points the way for our own ultimate victory over capitalist exploitation.

In the aftermath of this great celebration, peace activists must increase and extend popular opposition to U.S. policy in Central America. The Bush administration and Congress must be confronted with a determined mass movement that opposes U.S. interference in the upcoming Nicaraguan election. People must demand that the U.S. support, not try to scuttle, the Central American peace process as reflected in the Esquipulus, Sapoá, and Tela agreements. Concretely, this means completely disbanding the contras. Further, the solidarity movement must insist upon an end to the economic blockade of Nicaragua and to U.S. pressure on international financial institutions to veto Nicaraguan loan requests.

Peace and social justice in Nicaragua requires an end to U.S. efforts to control the entire region. Economic and military aid to the brutal government in El Salvador must cease. The U.S. militarization of Honduras has to stop. Most fundamentally, progressives must work to halt U.S. dominance in the region, allowing peoples there to determine their own futures.

In sum, growing numbers of workers, farmers, intellectuals and other progressive people in the USA and around the world have committed themselves to support the Nicaraguan revolution because they realize that, in an ultimate sense, it is one among the many revolutions for all of humanity. To this end, the U.S. policy of attempting to stamp out independent, progressive, anti-imperialist movements and governments must be defeated.